DIRT CHEAP VALUABLE

PREPPING

Cheap Stuff You Can Stockpile Now That Will Be Extremely Valuable When SHTF

By Cal Wilson

Dirt Cheap Valuable Prepping: Cheap Stuff You Can Stockpile Now That Will Be Extremely Valuable When SHTF

ISBN-13: 978-1508402091
ISBN-10: 1508402094

Table of Contents

Introduction

There are many good prepper "list" books out there. There are also some very good prepper fiction books that teach what items you should stockpile through fictional examples. This book is not one of either of those types of books. This book assumes you will *not* be able to stockpile everything you need in a worse-case scenario, and it suggests certain items to stockpile so that you can barter them for other items when the need arises. To put it another way, when it comes to stockpiling each and every item you need in a total SHTF situation, you can try but don't plan on having everything together when you need it. So stockpile what you can and barter for the rest.

And which items should we preppers stockpile? Simply the cheapest now that will be the most sought-after later. If you can see ahead and predict what items will be extremely valuable later, why not buy the cheapest ones right now?

Take salt, for example. As I write later in this book, salt is so cheap that it is the only item I am aware of that actually costs less than a dollar at the Dollar Store! You pay around fifty-four cents for a container of salt at the local Dollar Store, and what you are paying for is basically packaging and transportation. The salt itself costs almost nothing.

Yet salt will be used for all sorts of things in an SHTF scenario. You can use salt for cleaning, storing meat, preserving food, killing poison ivy or oak, spicing up your food; you can even use salt in a homemade toothpaste!

Or, what about athlete's foot and jock itch medicine? Two medicines that address very painful skin fungi in different parts of the body. Have you really thought about what things would be like in a true societal collapse? Thousands or even millions of people will be going months without bathing. Athlete's foot and jock itch will be rampant. There will be a lot of people out there who will be in excruciating pain, sometimes not even able to walk.

Yet today, athlete's foot and jock itch medicine are sold at the eighty-eight cent endcap at Walmart. It would be a great idea to stock up on both of these medicines. To someone who is suffering from these maladies, a person with athlete's foot and jock itch medicine can practically name their own price!

These and other items will be discussed, with suggestions for stockpiling. Why not stockpile stuff now that can be bought for next to nothing? But also the items will be explained as to why they will be important in a disaster or SHTF situation.

I will also include some testimonials that will reinforce the importance of the items I suggest stockpiling. Frankly, it is good to hear from people whose lives were saved by having on hand some of these items. It makes you feel a little different about the items and their importance.

You may also notice a big difference in the prepping approach in this book. Many people have watched the TV show *Doomsday Preppers*, and have had a good laugh at the people highlighted in that show because they base their preps on one specific disaster, and many times they are pretty unrealistic or downright silly. Some people on the show expect the north and south poles on the Earth to reverse, while others expect there to be a severe earthquake in the middle of the country. Some of the people featured expect more realistic things like a terrorist attack or a worldwide financial collapse. And another family planned a worldwide pandemic, and you never know if that family will get the last laugh.

First, the disasters I recommend you prepare for should be serious, not silly disasters. But more importantly, true preppers know that preparing for a specific, single disaster is folly. Like a person with an over-eating problem in a restaurant who hands the menu back to the waitress and says "OK," a true prepper prepares for anything and everything. No need to be choosy. Absolutely nothing is off the table. As preppers, we should prepare for a worldwide financial collapse, an earthquake in our area, a pandemic, a civil war, whatever. There is no reason why we should only prepare for a single specific disaster.

About the only line I draw is that disasters will probably not happen more than one at a time, although I am not exactly sure about that one either. Sure, I guess a worldwide financial crisis could happen while a pandemic spreads, but it is more likely that one or the other will happen. But, heck, why not plan on multiple disasters together? What would be the problem in that? It's not like you can be *over*-prepared. So you may have some extra supplies sitting around that you won't need. Who cares?

So in the pages that follow, this book will assume that the reader does not plan on any specific disaster. We will suggest preps for everything. A true "all of the above" approach to prepping!

Another thing: although it is not necessarily a barter item, one of the first chapters of this book will be on water because water is the weakest link in everyone's preparations. Simply put, nothing else matters if you don't have water taken care of. *Nothing*! You can have the most stored food, medication, guns and ammo, off-grid housing, and all the rest, but if you don't have your water situation worked out, you will be toast pretty soon.

The rest of the book is roughly organized in degrees of what I call *delta*. A delta in the context of this book is the difference between the cost of something now, and the value of the same item in the midst of a disaster or societal collapse. The higher the delta, the more towards the beginning of this book that items will be located. For example, salt, being almost free nowadays and very valuable after a collapse, will be listed first.

At the other end of the delta spectrum is what I call "regenerating things," so that is why these items are listed at the end of the book. For example, a chicken coup or an aquaponics system are pretty expensive right now, in fact they are quite a hassle, but they will be important is an SHTF situation. So regenerating things will be listed at the end.

Let's keep in mind the priorities of prepping in general. Water, food, shelter, heat, protection, medicine, communication, lighting are the most important needs in prepping. In storing up items that meet these needs, you should prioritize the items that cost the least now, but will be the most valuable in an SHTF situation.

Another thing: preppers have some basic rules, that I will repeat now, but I will include a caveat that no one else includes. I am referring to the "Rules of Three" that are repeated in most prepper books or TV shows. Here we go:

It takes about three minutes to die without air.
It takes about three hours to die without shelter (assuming horrible weather or something).
It takes about three days to die without water (but only two days without water before stupidity sets in).
It takes about three weeks to die without food (but only one week without food before stupidity sets in).
It takes about three months to die without hope (I'll try not to get political here).
And while we're talking about the number three, it is a good idea to have at least three ways of preventing a shortage of any of these basic commodities. (Kind of a backup of a backup).

The caveat I add here is morale, which is very important, and changes the basic rules. See, you can survive just fine after going without water for two days, for example, but your morale becomes awful and you start making mistakes and, in general, being stupid. So, although you may still survive, you make mistakes and may not survive for reasons other than lack of water.

That was a lesson I learned in an emergency a couple summers ago, when my family had to evacuate our neighborhood because of a fire. I kept the "Rules of Three" in mind and paced ourselves accordingly. But the funniest thing happened: my morale hit rock bottom and I started doing stupid things. If we weren't allowed back home, who knows how long I would have survived in this emergency? Probably not up to three days without water and up to three weeks without food.

So keep in mind the Rules of Three, but also give a little "fudge factor" regarding morale.

Two things you will notice that I have *not* included are firearms or ammo, and for good reason. In a post-collapse society, you might not know your barter partners well and may run the risk that they will use these items against you so that they can steal the rest of you stuff. So I would advise against bartering guns and ammo for that reason.

One last thing: many preppers approach the subject of prepping with a heavy heart, like you have to be in a sad mood to think about preparing and what to stock up on. I approach prepping with a good mood and a happy heart. When you think of it, we preppers have been let in on a secret that other people are totally unaware of. Well, everyone else except for the federal government, which is the world's biggest prepper. But that is a different issue.

But really, we preppers have been given a mindset, almost a vision, of how bad things will get someday, and we have the motivation to do something about it right now. Before the bottom drops out.

Ordinary people go about their lives, thinking things will always be stable and society will never collapse. The lights will always turn on and the tap water will always flow. When the sewage eventually hits the fan, boy, will they be surprised! We preppers have a head-start on them, and we should be glad!

So don't be surprised to be made aware of a totally different mindset in these pages. Frankly, we have a job to do, stocking up on cheap items that will be extremely valuable when things fall apart, and we should be happy while doing it! This is the smart way to do it, and this is an adventure!

I am happy while I prepare, and so should you. So, as they say in just about every YouTube video out there, "Let's get started, shall we?"

Salt

It's an old family joke of ours, and the kids are catching on. Every time we head to the Dollar Store, I ask someone "How much is that item right there?" and I point to something.

"One dollar," is the reply.

"How about that item?" and I point at another item.

"One dollar."

When we go through the check-out line, I helpfully offer to run and price-check on any item if the price is unknown. Our kids roll their eyes as the cashier looks confused.

Every once in a while I will catch someone off guard. "How much is that container of salt right there?" I ask, pointing at a container of salt.

"One dollar," someone says.

"Actually, if you look closely, you can see that it is only 54 cents," I say. And it is true: at the Dollar Store we go to, the containers of salt are only 54 cents – the cheapest item in the store!

"Got you there..." I announce the comedic payday.

All stores sell items for more than what the store pays for it. That is standard capitalism. And when something at even the Dollar Store sells for less than a dollar, you know that the item in question is extremely cheap. With salt, you are paying mostly for packaging and shipping. On its own, salt is practically free.

But salt has so many uses! For anyone who has eaten a lot of stored food like Mountain House, or MRE's, which I recommend you get used to eating, salt can add some taste to some otherwise bland food. Even boiled vegetables taste better, or at least have a taste, with a sprinkle of salt. To even the most basic stew or soup, salt adds great taste.

For anyone who has ever killed and field cleaned an animal to eat later, you know that salt is used to preserve the meat. Salt keeps the meat from spoiling as fast as it would spoil otherwise. Salt can also be part of a homemade Gatorade recipe, which is very important, and the subject of a different part of this book.

Salt can also be used in cleaning. Salt, mixed with twice as much baking soda (another dirt cheap product), is a great toothpaste.

Warm water with salt is a great mouthwash, and can get rid of mouth sores or sore throats. In fact, mixing water and salt was the norm for people who wanted relief from their sore throats for many years.

In case of a nasal congestion, salt can be used to make a saline nasal spray. Boil a cup of water, then let it cool, and add half a teaspoon of non-iodized salt and half a teaspoon of baking soda.

Salt can be used to deter ants. Just spread some salt around the outer boundary of a room.

Salt can be used to make a homemade "Round Up." If you mix salt with soap and water, the mixture and can be sprayed on plants to kill them. This will get rid of unwanted or dangerous plants like poison ivy or poison oak. In a setting where medicine and skin lotions will be very limited, preemptively killing harmful plants like that could be very important.

The same mixture, salt with soap and water, can be used as kind of a mildly-abrasive cleaning agent. This should be used on only the most stubborn stains on cookware or dishes, as the mixture, once used and washed off of whatever is being cleaned, will damage the soil it is dumped onto. So be careful with this blend.

Salt and water can also be used to alleviate the pain of insect bites. Apply a teaspoon of salt to the bite area and rub it in with a few drops of water.

What about iodized salt? Iodine is an essential mineral used by the body for growth and hormone regulation. Iodine deficiency, which caused an enlarged thyroid gland, a condition called goiter, used to be a major problem in the United States. So in the 1920's iodine was added in salt to make sure that people get at least the minimum amount needed. Iodine does not affect the taste of salt.

It is good to have at least some of your salt stores consist of iodized salt. And with the sea salt craze going strong, iodized salt is the cheapest available.

Every time you go to the grocery store, you should pick up an extra container of salt. Even at the most overpriced grocery stores, it won't add much to your total bill. Think of extra salt as a savings account for something that you can barter for other items in a longer-term disaster.

And, unlike many other items stored for SHTF, salt is pretty durable to store. So long as you keep it dry, salt has an unlimited shelf life and does not need to be kept below a certain temperature. So wherever you store all your preps, keep all your cooler areas for items other than salt. Salt can take the heat.

Spices

If you are like most preppers, you have a variety of Mountain House cans, MRE's and maybe other freeze-dried food stored away. As you should. If that type of food is good enough for the federal government to stockpile, then, by golly, it is good enough for us preppers too!

But have you ever really tasted the food we are storing? It is pretty bland! Hospital food tastes pretty zesty in comparison.

Salt will usually make bland food tastier, and other spices like garlic salt, cayenne pepper, Cajun and curry seasoning make a big difference with food that we store. Many of these spices are sold in the local Dollar Store, and will make a world of difference when all we have to eat is stored food. And because they have no liquids in them, they could last decades if properly stored in a cool, dark place. So stock up on as many of these spices as possible. Having a food with enough spices might make the difference between the food getting eaten or not.

The military is catching on, and it is trying to make MRE's no longer "meals rejected by Ethiopians," but rather a nice-tasting meal all on its own. MRE's nowadays even have an adorable, miniature bottle of Tabasco sauce. Yes, you read that right: it is cute! So sue me for being unmanly.

Anyway, listen to what a former Marine had to write on the subject of bland MRE's. He would know:

> Cal, in your prepper book, I hope you can emphasize the great benefit some simple spices and condiments can bring to Meals-Ready-to-Eat (MREs). Over the years I served in the Marine Corps, I lost track of how many individual and group MREs I ate. I know campers and preppers

sometimes make an MRE and are surprised how edible it is. Perhaps an MRE could be fine when you are excited about the meal, such as lasagna, and you can have the time to combine and heat all the ingredients, and it's just one small speed bump in an otherwise healthy diet.

However, when it is the staple of your diet or you can't take the time to prepare it fully, even MREs grow old very quickly.

Let me tell you about one meal I had in Afghanistan. I had barely slept in several days while my team retrograded, or disassembled, a small Marine Corps base. After our retrograde convoy arrived at the destination base, I had to stand duty at night, watching over trucks and gear while most of the team slept. I remember discovering that my meal was a really nauseating "omelet" MRE. In that exposed and exhausted state, I ate maybe a single one hundred-calorie item and threw out the rest. I have seen the same thing happen many times in training or on deployment; troops trashing or skipping unpalatable meals. Then they grow tired, irritable, and lose mental power. I have even seen an over-exerted commander compulsively vomit from lack of sustenance.

Inedible or dull MREs are a significant problem in combat or in the disaster scenarios for which preppers plan. In fact, the military is investing heavily in making the meals more palatable and portable. So while one day MREs may be as delicious as they are nutritious, in the meantime, I encourage preppers everywhere to stock up on seasonings. On a deployment, the most valuable care package items are hot sauces, relishes, flavored sandwich spreads, and similar condiments. In my opinion, preppers would be wise to stock as much variety of spices and condiments as possible to help make prepackaged meals more palatable.

--Capt. Patrick Timmons, USMC 2009 – 2014

Water

With the exception of air, water is the most critical ingredient in staying alive. Water is almost always a prepper's weakest link. Unless you are blessed to live on land that has a running stream or a water well, obtaining, filtering and storing water will be your main preoccupation in keeping yourself alive. You should take this issue very seriously.

This might seem out of place in a book about being cheap with preps, but let me say this: don't be cheap with water and water-related preps. Obtaining water, filtering it and storing it is extremely important to survival.

First, if there is a well-announced collapse or something that happens, and you have a few minutes to prepare, it would be a great idea to hook up a "waterBOB" to your bathtub and fill it up with water. This thing sells for $25 on Amazon, fits any bathtub, will hold up to 100 gallons of water, and the water will be cleaner than water just filled up in your bathtub. It will keep the water fresh for up to 12 weeks. These things also come with a small siphon pump to disperse the water into jugs or pitchers.

I have also been impressed with the "water brick," which is a 3.5 gallon container made to store potable water. These things sell for about $30, and because they are only 3.5 gallons, most people can carry them when they are full of water. And the handle that attaches to the water brick is also very sturdy and comfortable to carry. These are made out of very thick, food-grade plastic, so you can buy and stack many of these things.

Another thing you can use to store water, which I also discuss in the chapter on trash later in this book, is the gallon-sized container of water sold by Crystal Geyser. These are the clear plastic, one-gallon size jugs that have a handle that is kind of taped to the top of it. They have a screw-top lid, so the container can be used and reused many times. And the plastic looks like it is strong enough to last a while. Crystal Geyser is probably not the only brand that does this, so keep your eyes open for other one-gallon jugs of water that are made of solid plastic and have a screw-top lid.

Water bricks and these one-gallon containers can be used if you are away from home and a close water source. If you can find a water source, like a spring or a creek, you can fill up one of these containers with the water from that source. But before you drink it, make sure to either filter it, or boil it, or treat the water with bleach so that you kill any of the bacteria or pathogens that come with water.

Any time you try to store water and keep it problem-free, make sure to put eight drops of regular household bleach into every gallon of water. For the water brick discussed above, that translates to 28 drops of bleach. If you cover up the water, that amount of added bleach will keep it clean for a year.

Filtering the water is extremely important, and you should make sure to have filtering supplies on hand. The cheapest filters on the market are probably coffee filters. While these things were made for coffee, they can also be used to filter out a lot of harmful stuff in water that you have collected.

There is another item on the market that I feel is a little overpriced, but it is good. It is the Life Straw, which normally sells for about $20 apiece. It looks just like a very thick, light blue plastic straw, and you are supposed to lay down on the banks of a creek a suck water through it to drink. You could also scoop up some creek water into a cup and suck the water to drink out of the cup. I have used the Life Straw and I feel good about including it in my preps.

But when you are thirsty and crave water, it is kind of unappetizing to suck water out of a straw. Katadyn make a pretty good water filter/hand pump that you could use to filter water form one cup and put the clean water into another cup and drink it that way. But these things are also expensive. Katadyn filters sell from $75, up to $500 apiece, depending on the model. Katadyn also sells many replacement parts for their filters.

For years I have owned several of the 22-ounce Sport Berkey Water Filter Bottles, and I am very happy with them. They are a light blue plastic bottle that you keep water inside and suck through a water straw that brings the water up through a filter. And when you are done drinking the water, you can fold the top down and the straw part of it is concealed. These things filter out about 99% of harmful pathogens out of the water, including E.coli, which has found its way into some municipal water supplies in the past. The bottle even comes with a carry handle, so that you can attach it to a backpack if needed. The Sport Berkey Water Filter Bottle usually sells for $19 apiece, and the replacement filter sells for $17, and they can be bought at Amazon, or at Directive 21.

There is a competitor named Sawyer that sells a similar product. In fact, it looks like the same thing, for $30. So far, I have heard good reviews of it, but I am still sold on Berkey.

Berkey makes a household-size filter, called a "Big Berkey," and it kind of looks like a stainless steel water cooler. It would work for a whole household. They cost several hundred dollars, but they work great. The idea is to bring a lot of water to it, by carrying some water in from a stream or other water source, and then pour the water into the top of the Big Berkey. It slowly filters the water, then you can get some water from the spigot at the bottom. The replacement parts are important, so if you buy one of these, make sure to also stock up on filters.

Berkey is a great water-filtration company. I have heard of people mixing food coloring into water and then running it through a Berkey filter, and the water comes out clear. Also, if you have municipal water and it has a slight chlorine smell, you can drink the water through a Berkey filter and the water will no longer have the smell.

So get to know all of these water filtration products. Keep many of them in your house or retreat location, and make sure that you have more of these and their replacement parts than you will ever need. Know how to use them. Again, water is extremely important. Without water taken care of, nothing else matters. You can have the most stored food, weapons, first aid supplies, and clothing shelter, but without water taken care of, it doesn't matter. In a longer-term collapse, you will not survive. It is that simple.

Athlete's Foot And Jock Itch Creams

A few months ago my daughter and I were in our backyard hot tub, and a water fight broke out. Water flew everywhere, including my bathrobe, towels and slippers that were nearby. When things settled down and we went back inside the house to watch a movie on TV, I stayed in my partially-wet bathrobe and slippers, not thinking much of it. The next day I had a horrible, painful fungus on my right foot. I could barely walk! An overseas trip I was scheduled take was in jeopardy.

After four days of smearing this athlete's foot cream on my foot, the fungus died off and I was able to walk again.

For anyone who has ever participated in high school or college sports, you know the extreme pain that can be caused by jock itch, which is another skin fungus. It is also difficult to walk with jock itch. You learn the hard way of the importance of constant bathing.

Even if you are not participating in sports, jock itch attacks men and women alike. All it takes is a few days of skipping a bath or shower.

But think of it: in a true, societal collapse, thousands or even millions of people will not be able to change clothes, bathe or stay clean. If they walk through water, they will be walking in wet shoes for a while. They will not be able to clean up, dry off and keep their feet from getting athlete's foot. Fully functioning showers and bath tubs will be extremely rare, so jock itch will also be rampant. That will be a lot of people out there, totally in pain.

I bought the athlete's foot cream that cured my athlete's foot at Walmart, at an eighty-eight cent endcap in the pharmacy section. Eight-eight cents is all it took to bring me from agony to relief.

This is a very important thing to stockpile up on. Both athlete's foot and jock itch cream – it is a skin fungus either way – should be repeatedly bought and stocked up on. I have a five-gallon buckets filled with tubes of these creams, and I feel like I should beginning another one.

This stuff is a prime example of stuff that is extremely cheap now, but will be extremely valuable if the sewage hits the fan and society collapses. Can you imagine how valuable these creams will be to people -- and there will be many -- who are suffering from these ailments? Yet, as valuable as this stuff will be in those later days, athlete's foot and jock itch creams are very, very cheap right now.

So begin your stockpile of this stuff right now! And keep it in a cool, dry place.

Where To Get Stuff

Sometimes preppers spend a lot of money on their preps! In fact, that is a usual rookie prepper mistake. And, obviously, the less you spend on your preps, the more you can buy. So choosy shopping is very important.

Here are some ideas on where you should buy your preps: Salvation Army, Goodwill (and its online store, shopgoodwill.com), Walmart, Sam's Club, BJ's, Fred Meyer, Ross Stores, garage sales, Ebay, Amazon, and the various specialty online prepper stores that are out there.

And watch for sales, everywhere you go. Hardware stores usually have sales in the fall to get rid of their summer garden tools. That would be a great time to stock up on shovels, hand tools, axes and hatchets. Walmart has an eighty-eight cent endcap in its pharmacy, where they sell all sorts of medications that you can stock up on. Even the Dollar Store has some items that are put up for clearance every once in a while.

Ebay has some great deals on both used and new things. Here is something I did recently, at the suggestion of James Rawles: I did an Ebay search for "TSA," which is an auction of stuff confiscated by the TSA at airports. Apparently there are many stupid people who try to go through security checkpoints with pocket knives and multi-tools. Be prepared to spend $60 or more for 20-30 pocket knives and multi-tools. I won one of these auctions and one of the multi-tools I bought had "National Guard" imprinted on the side, which was cool.

Craig's List occasionally lists free stuff, just given away. A friend of mine picked up a pick-up truck full of Mountain House #10 cans of freeze-dried food that the new owner of a house was just giving away, to clear out a basement. Totally free! My friend is now one of the best-prepared friends I have, and he got the bulk of his preps for free!

Addictions

If you have ever been truly addicted to something, you know the control the addition has over someone. There are three main legally-addictive things that people can store: coffee, cigarettes, and alcohol. This stuff will be great for storing and bartering. And they all fit neatly into five gallon buckets.

In my stockpile of coffee, I have those Tasters Choice "serve sticks" that are designed to be used in 6 ounces of hot water. The price is OK, and the taste is actually pretty good. I buy the medium roast Colombian, but I have heard that the hazelnut and vanilla choices are excellent. The only catch I have found is that you need to double-up with these for a normal cup of coffee. If you serve it as instructed, the coffee will taste a little watery.

Nevertheless, it is excellent and you will be pleasantly surprised at how good instant coffee has come since the early days.

Starbucks also has a good version of the "serve sticks" with its "Via" brand, but it is very expensive. If you are trying to store up a lot of this stuff, you can almost go broke buying Starbucks instant coffee.

Either way, I prefer the "sticks" method of instant coffee containers instead of a jar full of the stuff that you spoon coffee out of. Serving sticks seem to be a better way to store it. A single serving stick of this instant coffee could be easily traded, and you know the correct amount that you are pouring in your hot water. I have no idea of the shelf life, but it is probably a long time, as there is not much in the way of liquids and oils in these sticks.

With my coffee preps I have bought a bunch of the packets of Coffee Mate creamer, and Splenda. Although, let's face it, in a true long-term survival, staying away from sugar will not be a high priority, so you might as well store up some packets of real sugar.

A couple sticks of instant coffee, two packets of creamer, two packets of sugar would probably be a great group of items to barter with when the need arises.

But however you do it, I can imagine how welcomed it would be for someone who has gone without coffee for a while to boil some water and mix some of this instant coffee in, and top it off with creamer and sugar.

Cigarettes are also great to store up, because they will be excellent barter items someday. Have you ever really noticed anyone who smokes cigarettes, and how they practically climb the wall after a few hours without a smoke? This addiction is extremely powerful.

I keep a look out for sales on cigarettes whatever store I go. I doubt the brand of the cigarette will be that important, and cigarettes that have an unknown brand are a lot cheaper than Marlboro or Camel. Friends of mine who smoke have told me that occasionally it is good to have a menthol cigarette, so I also have a few of those stored away too. In the same fiver gallon bucket that I have my cigarettes stored in, I include a lot of those cheap matches and Bic lighters. That way, if I ever barter a cigarette or two, I can also offer to light the cigarette for the customer. I feel like my stored cigarettes are practically money in the bank for a societal collapse.

As with the stored coffee serving sticks, I have no idea what the shelf life of cigarettes is. However, it has to be pretty long. There are no liquids or oils in cigarettes, and cigarettes are used by burning them and inhaling the smoke from them. So the shelf life of cigarettes is probably a long time.

I also have a stockpile of small bottles of vodka. Why vodka, and not gin or rum? Vodka has a fairly neutral taste, and has a higher percent of alcohol so that it can also be used for fires. The plastic bottles I buy are small and durable, and be easily transported and poured.

Containers

All of the stuff you stockpile needs to be stored somewhere. You cannot just leave this stuff out in your garage or in an attic somewhere. This stuff needs to be stored in containers, if for no other reason than to keep it all straight. Containers also help with moving your stored stuff. Here are some ideas for storage:

Freezer-grade baggies, both quart and gallon size. The two-gallon size is also nice, but is not needed as much. These are fairly cheap at Walmart and other grocery stores, and freezer-grade baggies are important. You can store many different things in these baggies. If they are freezer-grade then they will be sturdier and last longer. When you have used one of these, instead of throwing them away, wash them out and dry them where you dry the dishes you have just cleaned. Avoid the baggies with the little plastic "slider" thingy because in time those things will break off.

13-gallon kitchen bags, often sold with drawstrings, are good to keep and store. You can pack up and transport just about anything in these things. I have never cleaned one of them, but that is probably possible.

Contractor bags: these are 55-gallon bags that are very sturdy. They can carry and store sharp items and there is a lower chance that something will poke through. In a pinch, you could fill a contractor bag with leaves and use it as a makeshift mattress that will insulate you from the cold ground when you are sleeping outside.

Five-gallon buckets. These are rarely over $5 apiece at hardware stores, and sometimes you can even talk a restaurant into giving you their old five-gallon, food-grade buckets for free. The lids you usually buy at hardware stores for these can crack or break, and I am not very impressed with them. I usually spend $15 apiece on Amazon for gamma seal lids that can be much easier opened and closed, and they will last much longer. Home Depot sells black gamma seal lids for $7 apiece. When you start to build up a collection of these, it is a good idea to put some duct tape on the front and write the contents of the bucket on the duct tape.

One thing that I have stored in some five-gallon buckets is freezer-grade baggies.

Five-gallon buckets can be stored above or buried below ground. There are problems in burying these things, as they are not always watertight, and it is difficult to bury them and then unbury them. You will need to dig up and clear the entire top of the bucket before you can pull it out of the ground, and this is a hassle.

I just recently came across a smaller bucket with some additions, and they are called Monovaults. These are made for burying, and the top lid is made to protect from water. It is about the size to store a pistol and nothing else. The thing is pretty expensive, $80 on Amazon.

A little more practical is the MTM Survivor Ammo Can Underground Storage Cache SAC, which is the size of a five-gallon bucket. It costs $30 on Amazon, and it looks like it keeps things pretty watertight and secure.

Cache tubes, also known as "Survival Cache" tubes are things that you can build yourself. As with anything you bury, the main advantage is a cooler temperature, which matters with things like medications and foods. Large-scale storage in cooler temperatures, like a root cellar, is much more expensive.

Cache tubes are basically plastic pipes (PVC or ABS) that you buy at a hardware store, cut to about two or three feet long, and glue an end cap on one end, and then a cleanout adapter (the screw-off end) on the other side. They are narrower, because 4-inch diameter is the biggest diameter you can buy, so there is not too much that can fit inside. But they are easier to bury and better at keeping water out. (Actually that is not always true. I once bought an 8-inch

PVC pipe and glued the appropriate ends on it, and when all was said and done, the cost was about $80 per cache tube!)

Whenever you bury anything, if you bury something metallic (like for example a knife, some ammo, silver coins or a can opener), make sure to throw some small nuts and bolts on the ground, to throw off anyone with a metal detector looking for your stuff.

Of course, you should keep track of where you bury your cache tubes. Main advantages to burying things that you stockpile include secrecy and temperature control. Things are buried are usually kept at a pretty steady 55 degrees Fahrenheit.

With anything you bury, whether it is in a cache tube or five-gallon bucket, make sure that what you bury is water-tight. If you are unsure, you should enclose the items inside the tube inside freezer-grade baggies.

Shipping containers: A friend of ours recently paid $2,500 for a 20-foot long container, delivered. 40-foot long containers are also available. As opposed to other containers, my friend's container was in good shape. It is a good idea to personally check your container before you buy it and have it delivered. Rust and damages might make a container not last so long, or fall apart in time. If you are inspired to buy one of these, keep in mind that they have no shelves inside, and they lack ventilation. So if you buy one, make sure to keep several shelves inside.

Some people have tried buying these containers and then burying them (except for the doors), so that they are hidden and temperature-controlled. And they are right, the shelf life of stored items is greatly extended when the temperature is lower. But this is probably not a good idea. Sure, the containers are made to support up to six or eight other containers on top, but the weight is uniform and placed on frames. Burying dirt on containers places weight on the sides and top -- places that are not designed to take pressure. If a top of a container is buried and the soil becomes wet, there is nowhere for the water to go. So the container top develops rust and water eventually starts leaking into the container.

Eventually mud and water start accumulating inside the container and it becomes a huge mess.

And the dirt on the side of a buried container will press against the container's side so that the side eventually bows towards the inside.

Another thing about containers: I have always been suspicious of containers that people have way out in the country. What happens if you go inside and the wind blows the door shut? It is possible to have a door slammed shut and the locking mechanism will fall into place, so you might find yourself trapped inside. If this happens to you, and you don't have your cell phone on you, or if you are in an area that does not have cell phone coverage, you could be screwed. So be careful with shipping containers.

Here is one of my five gallon buckets, with a gamma seal lid. Notice the duct tape on the side that shows the contents of the bucket, in this case Ziplock gallon-size baggies.

Junk Land

A lot of preppers have the idea that it is good to stockpile "junk silver," dimes and quarters that are minted before 1965, and they are right. If the end comes, these coins will be something you can have on hand to actually buy stuff you need.

But I would like to encourage you to buy "junk land," which is raw land that is cheap and plentiful, and out in the country. Realtors call it "raw land" because it is a parcel of land and nothing is there, not even roads, electricity or water. Many times the owner has inherited this land, or a larger parcel has been divided and parts of it are put up for sale. Despite the number of acres that make up the size of the property, the land is sometimes hard to sell and the owner will offer to finance the purchase for you.

Raw land is a prepper's dream! If the sewage really hit the fan, where else can you go to survive but in the country? And with several acres under your control, you can plant food, forage for food, store some supplies, hunt, live, and survive.

The way you find this raw land is to locate an area outside of a suburban area, sometimes 100 or more miles away, and do a Google search for the terms "raw land" "acreage" and "owner finance." You will be amazed at the numbers of acres available for sale at relatively low prices.

It will be a different experience for people who were born and raised in cities. People who have spent most of their lives in cities will figure that 50 – 100 acres of land will cost millions of dollars. And they are right, so long at the land is surrounded by neighborhoods and roads! But if you look closely, you can find this much land for sale, for low prices, out in the country.

Part of the reason for the low prices on acreage in the country is because the land is pretty inaccessible to where people want to live and work. So much the better! To survive a true SHFT situation, you want to have land that is far away from where people live and work; far away from interstate highways. This is truly un-glamorous, tucked-away, mostly inaccessible land that no one wants. When hordes of people march out of the cities to look for food and farms to take over, they will mostly stick to the interstate highways, and the further your property is from one of these, the better.

Here are some priorities I suggest in your search for junk land: make sure it is a big piece of land, preferably 20 acres or more. With 20 acres or more, you may be able to go truly unnoticed by the neighbors or travelers nearby. Being unnoticed is very important.

Once you buy the land, explore it. Bring some saws and pruning shears and cut a hiking trail into the middle of your property. If your land is hilly, find a flat area. In time, your hiking trail will become worn, and someday you can hire a local bulldozer operator to come onto your land and turn your hiking trail into a small road that you can drive on. Make sure there are some "turn around" areas adjacent to the road, and you will need to hire local people to come to your property and spread some gravel so that you don't get stuck or slide off the road when it rains.

The thing to keep in mind about gravel is that once it is spread out on your roads, you need to drive on it after it gets wet and then apply another layer of gravel. And after it rains again, maybe a third layer of gravel! Eventually the gravel will be packed in tight, and the road will be just as secure as if it were paved. Also, make sure that you have some water ditches on each side of the roads, so that your roads do not get washed away in a heavy rainstorm.

Water is also very important. Ideally, the land would have a running stream, but if that is not available, consider having a water well drilled uphill from any possible building site. Ask the neighbors how successful they have been in drilling wells that produce water. Usually parcels of land that are near each other will have similar water well issues.

I had some success in hiring a "douser," or a "water witch," to come to our property and find areas that would be good bets to dig a well. As a Christian, the term "witcher" annoyed me, but a person who does this work does not engage in witchcraft but instead measures changes in magnetic attractions from one step on your property to another. If the magnetism changes abruptly, the person figures that this is an area that would be good to dig a water well.

It worked on our property. We hired a water well driller to dig a water well (costing us about $9,000) at one of the locations the douser had selected. The well-driller dig down about 200 feet, and our well was tested to produce seven gallons of water per minute. The well driller "cased" the hole with PVC pipe and we hired someone else to put in a hand-powered water well pump, and that cost less than $1,000. At some point in the future we will address the "hardness" of the water, which is a measure of various minerals in the water, but the water is still drinkable.

One issue in buying raw land is that the land should, if affordable, be surveyed, so that you know where the boundaries of the land are. This can be pretty expensive, especially with larger parcels of land whose boundaries will go through dense forest. If the survey job costs way too much money, it still might be possible to compare notes with the neighbor on the approximate land boundaries.

Another issue with buying raw land in the country is that many times the land in question is land-locked. That might be why that 100 acres lot, for example, only a few miles outside of a small town, with beautiful rolling hills, in so cheap. I have actually heard horror stories of people buying property out in the country, which is beautiful and just a short hike through the neighbor's land. Eventually, "no trespassing" sign go up, lawyers' letters are mailed telling the land-locked land owner to stay off of the land between a road and the destination property, and the land-locked land truly becomes inaccessible and worthless. A face-to-face meeting with the neighbor results in no permission to get to the land-locked land,

and the phrase "you should have thought about this when you bought the land" is spoken. Truly a nightmare!

However, a good prepper should view land-locked land as an opportunity, not a setback. Ultimately, your goal will be to buy a permanent "easement road" from your neighbor so that you can drive from a local road, through your neighbor's property, to your land so that it is no longer land-locked. This can be tricky, but it is doable. The extra hassle in getting an easement road explains the lower price of land-locked properties.

Before buying some land-locked land, you will need to approach the neighbor who owns the land between the land-locked property and the road, and ask to buy an option to purchase an easement road through their land. Of course, an offer for money will be involved, and the land-owner may know that they have you at a disadvantage. But sometimes the neighbor will have a contracting or construction company that you can offer to hire to work on the road once you own the land and have the easement. Or there might be some other enticements you can offer.

In some jurisdictions you can offer to trade some land with the neighbor, and this is called a "lot line adjustment," so that you could own a stretch of land between the land-locked property and a nearby road, and your neighbor will get the same area of the land-locked property in exchange. This solution to a land-locked property might be something that no one has ever thought of.

In either case, an option to buy an easement, or an option to do a lot-line adjustment, you must have this in hand before you actually buy the land-locked property. If you don't have this taken care of before you buy the land, it could be too late. The owner of the land between your property and the road will know that he or she has a serious upper hand with you.

The details of getting an option to buy an easement, and the legalities of it all are outside the scope of this book, and I am not here to give you real estate legal advice. But just keep in mind that it is possible to turn a land-locked property into an accessible property, and doing so may only be a hurdle or two away. Educate yourself on the local easement laws, find a local real estate attorney and tell him or her your goals, and go for it. It is possible that you could buy some land that really is valuable but no one else wanted because of the accessibility issues. But be careful.

Once you own the land, familiarize yourself with the local county rules for developing, building roads, drilling wells, building structures, and leaving vehicles there. In talking with county officials, your attitude should be "I want to comply with the rules," but it is a good idea to keep your specific plans to yourself. I remember once speaking with someone at my county's building permit office, and I asked about some rules about building a structure smaller than is required to get a permit. "Hey, be careful what you do," he sneered at me. "If we find out where your property is and that you have built something against the rules without a permit, you will have repercussions." I answered, "That's why I am here asking you what the rules are."

You should also keep track of your property, and you should fence off your property so that hikers don't wander onto your property and get injured and sue you. Also – and I have never seen this but I have heard of it – a property that has no fences could find itself explored by local county officials, looking for code violations.

Any workers you hire to come to the property and do work should be scrutinized. They will probably realize that this is property that is vacant most of the time, so they could always come back later, when you aren't there, and help themselves to whatever is there. I had a couple of generators stolen, and I strongly suspect a couple of the workers I hired to come by to do some work. Since then I have built sheds that are burglar-proof, and I keep my generators and tools there.

As you get more experienced with your property you will find that you have all sorts of things that are left there, and they are liable to the stolen if they are not secured. Costco sells a pretty cheap shed that can be locked. In some areas, a small wooden shed can be bought and the seller will construct it for you at the area you choose.

Possibly the best and cheapest structure you can put on your property is a either a used RV or a school bus. I have been amazed at how cheap old RV's and school buses are on Ebay. Either one could be bought for very little money, and parked in an area that is not easily seen outside the property. Then the RV or school bus should be painted dark green or tan camouflage, depending on the terrain. Then it could the locked to secure your tools and other valuables, and you will have a quick and easy place to stay once you get on to your property.

A front gate is also important, and there is a company called Mighty Mule that sells battery-operated front gate openers that can be installed and powered by solar panels. They work great, and they are available at Tractor Supply stores. In some jurisdictions, you must post "no trespassing" signs before you can get the police to prosecute anyone found trespassing on your property.

But it all starts with finding raw land at a price that you can afford. Here are some websites that I have found that list raw land for sale, and sometimes the properties are offered with owner financing:

You can check out the website Survival Realty for some ideas, but keep in mind these houses are mostly for millionaire preppers who don't mind if their prepper location has already been publicized everywhere. In my opinion this is just not very realistic. But the website is still interesting, and generates ideas of what a good, if overdone prepper location is like.

There are many others, but here are some other websites that list raw land, some of which are offered with owner-financing:

Countryplacesinc.com – Tennessee, Alabama and Kentucky
Billyland.com – western USA
Inlandproperties.com – northern SF Bay Area
Hillcountryrealestate.net – TX Hill Country

Landsofmissouri.com – Missouri
Floridaland1.com – central Florida land
Landsofmontana.com – Montana land

Trash

Have you ever taken a good look at what you throw away? Chances are that there are several items that you throw away all the time that will come in pretty handy in a disaster situation. Examining your trash before it gets picked up by the trash truck would be a great idea. You could find a treasure trove of stuff that would be usable if times get hard.

One idea of a useful trash item is the small soft drink container, usually Diet Coke, that is made of food-grade plastic and the bottle seems much thicker than is needed for one use of soft drink. I mean really, these are the type of plastic bottles that I could see lasting several hundred years in a landfill somewhere! They would be an excellent container to store stuff in, food-related or not.

I do a similar thing with a 2-liter size soft drink container. Once our family finishes with the Diet Coke, or root beer, or whatever, I clean and dry the bottle, then fill it up with dried beans of some sort. I have some of these storing lentil beans, splits peas, pinto beans, and even Cajun-flavored rice and beans. If there are some instructions on the packet, or a seasoning packet that comes with the mix, I tape all that onto the outside of the bottle. Then I make sure to write the year that I put this together, and store it in the back of a closet or pantry. I don't know the shelf life of these, but because they are dried, the shelf life has to be a long time if kept in a cool, dry place.

The unit cost is very low, probably less than six dollars per bottle. This would be a great item to over-stock on and use for barter someday.

Another idea of something that is extremely valuable that most people routinely throw away is dryer lint. Dryer lint is the perfect kindling. In our household, we keep a plastic bag hanging up nearby the dryer, and we collect all of the lint that we clean out of our dryer whenever we do our laundry. When the bag is filled up with lint, we seal it off and store it in a gallon-sized baggie.

This stuff is great! A few months ago we had a firearms club meeting and the members of the club were comparing our emergency bags and the contents inside. I showed everyone my magnesium fire-starter, those things that shoot off sparks, and baggie-full of dryer lint (packed separately). No one believed that this stuff could quickly start a fire.

So I grabbed a handful of the dryer lint, and my magnesium fire starter and headed out the door to the patio. I put the lint on the ground and jabbed the magnesium fire starter into in, and on the first try, a small fire started, right there! The rest of the group had still not made it out of the house! People couldn't believe it. By popular demand, I demonstrated this quick fire-starter several more times. I don't think a Bic lighter could have been quicker.

One other thing I want to mention as far as trash that could be reused in an SHTF-situation is the gallon-sized container of water sold by Crystal Geyser. These are the clear plastic, one-gallon size jugs that have a handle that is kind of taped to the top of it. Those bottles have a screw-top lid, so the container can be used and reused many times, not only to carry water, but anything else edible, like soup. There is no reason to throw these things away. And the plastic looks like it is strong enough to last a while.

Here is an example of some of the used bottles I have saved from the trash, cleaned and dried, then filled up with dried beans and split peas. I have taped the instructions and seasoning packages on the outside, and marked the year that I did this. The unit cost for any one of these is less than six dollars, and could feed a family of four for probably a couple days.

Used Blankets, Coats And Sleeping Bags

Every winter, you see the news reports of homeless shelters and how they cannot house all the homeless people who are out on the streets, trying to survive in very cold weather. In the last one I saw, the person who ran the homeless shelter reported of rampant pneumonia, and urged all of the homeless people to go to the local Goodwill and Salvation Army stores and pick up some used blankets, coats and sleeping bags. Homeless people were living outside in the cold without cover! The news reporter then urged us viewers to donate these same items to the Goodwill and Salvation Army stores so that they can be bought by the homeless people.

If you think about it, with a truly SHTF situation, depending on the particular disaster, many of us preppers could become homeless people. For whatever reason, our homes or our whole region of the country may be uninhabitable. That could be us, living outside and freezing, catching pneumonia, if we aren't warm and dry. Blankets, coats and sleeping bags are very important to have stocked up, ready to use when needed. They could save our life!

Another thing to consider: blankets, coats and sleeping bags are extremely expensive when they are brand new. The wife and I were recently invited to join another family on a camping trip, and I checked the local REI store, and was amazed to find sleeping bags, made of down and tested to withstand zero degree temperatures, selling for $200 on up! What a rip-off! I quickly checked Ebay and bought a used, military sleeping bag for $25 and no one knew the difference.

The sleeping bag that I bought on Ebay seemed brand new to me. And that makes sense. The likelihood of buying a "used" sleeping bag that is really new, but used maybe two or three times, is pretty high.

I checked, and used coats made of down are a similar savings on Ebay. Not as great a savings, but close.

But the point is that there is no need to start looking for new coats or sleeping bags, when used ones are available on Ebay for much, much less.

Same for blankets. I was recently shopping in Ross and noticed a pretty good savings on blankets there. Of course, they were sorted by color and style, which is irrelevant in a disaster. These blankets, and the used coats and sleeping bags for that matter, could be life-savers.

As for blankets, I have a natural affinity for 100% wool, but after comparing prices, I am now sold on fleece. Fleece is almost a miracle fabric, as it is cheap and very warm. The only problem I have found with fleece so far is that it is difficult to dye. So if you find a great deal on a fleece blanket that is yellow and pink, maybe with a "Hello Kitty" design on it, you might be stuck with it, as is.

Sewing Supplies

Things breaking down and breaking apart is a certainty. That is why it is so important to stockpile manual tools, as opposed to generators and anything else with a gas or electric motor. But clothing, tents, sleeping bags, backpacks and anything else made of fabric will surely get rips and holes in them. Keeping a supply of sewing supplies and mini kits will enable you to repair these items.

And it is nice that small sewing kits are so cheap. I found one on Amazon for only $7. And the kit I found had a nylon case that, unlike a plastic case, could be pushed into a small space in a backpack without breaking.

And another thing: keep in mind that just about no one else will have items like this stored up, so having a few extras on hand will be something you can barter with. There will be a demand for this stuff.

Hard Candy

This may be sounding like a commercial for Dollar Stores, but in this case, there is no better deal than to stock up on the small bags of hard candy that cost you only $1 apiece. If it is hard candy, the shelf life is extremely long, possibly indefinite. Make sure you do not include M&M's or anything else that has chocolate in it. In fact, if you, like me, accidentally buy some chocolate candies, it is best to just eat them and finish them off right now, so that they don't accidentally get packed away in your preps. You don't want to see stuff like that go to waste, you know. There are starving people out there in the world!

And if the package of hard candy is small enough, like what is sold in the Dollar Stores, it is very easy to barter away.

Flashlights, Rechargeable Batteries, Chargers

Let's face it: in case of an extended disaster, we will be living out in the country among the animals. Animals spend their nights looking for other animals or humans to eat.

Or, figure this: in case of an extended disaster, we will be surviving out in the country, while many thousands or even millions of people will be leaving the cities and will want to take what we preppers have to support ourselves and our families. Whether we need to defend ourselves against animals trying to eat us, or humans trying to take over our preps, it will be the post-apocalyptic version of survival of the fittest.

Flashlights are key. At nighttime, a good flashlight will dazzle the eyes of animals and humans alike, giving you the instant upper hand to defend yourself, or to kill the animal for food.

In flashlights: look for high lumens, and make sure the batteries used are either AA or AAA. The brand of the flashlight doesn't really matter. A few months ago I was sold on the brand Dorcy, which sold a 190-lumen flashlight for $20 on Amazon. Then I was walking through a Costco one day and saw that Duracell had three 300-lumen batteries on sale for $30! Once I made sure that the Duracell flashlights used AA batteries, I was sold. So buy a few high-lumen, AA or AAA-powered flashlights; many more than you will need.

Another advantage to having a properly-charged flashlights is that they will also allow you to do work during the night that you would otherwise have to be done in the daytime. Sometimes that makes a difference. But don't take my word for it. Here is a testimonial from a Marine who can tell you the importance of flashlights when you are in hostile territory:

> Cal, in your essential prepper items book, I hope you stress how important flashlights and rechargeable batteries can be. Let me tell you about an incident that occurred to me in Afghanistan when I was deployed in the Marine Corps in 2013.
>
> I was the logistics officer in small team of 20 Marines, stationed at a Forward Operating Base (FOB), with an Afghan military unit that we were training, deep inside Taliban-controlled territory. We Americans lived in one building that contained security cameras, lights, radios, and even computers in our small office. Everything at the base was powered by two diesel fuel generators. One day I was working in our small office when all the lights and computers switched off. Thirty seconds later, one of my Marines threw open the door and shouted to me, "We got a problem, Sir!" He quickly led me outside to the generators, which were burning, smoking, and spurting burning hot oil onto the ground.
>
> I quickly found a back-up radio and contacted our headquarters unit, which was 100 kilometers away. Luckily they were able to immediately fly two new generators out via helicopter to a nearby British base for us to retrieve via convoy. In an operation that lasted throughout the night, half our team remained on high alert at our powerless FOB, guarding against a possible attack, while the other half took vehicles to pick up the generators.
>
> Through all the loading, transportation, unloading, and installation of these new generators, the most

impactful tools we had were our flashlights. Using rechargeable batteries, our small flashlights enabled us to maintain a temporary perimeter when our security systems were down and were essential in working through the night both with heavy equipment and in small control panels. Several weeks before this incident, we had received a care package from a non-profit called Lights For Marines. They gave every team member a compact Foursevens Quark Pro flashlight, which was uniquely useful in that it has a clip built in to be easily affixed to a hat brim, enabling us to illuminate the area in front of us while keeping our hands free.

Luckily, we were not attacked that vulnerable night in Helmand Province, and we were back online in the morning. Our flashlights and rechargeable batteries may have saved our FOB that night, and I continue to use and value my flashlight now that I'm safe stateside. I hope your prepper readers think critically about the similar needs they will have if disaster strikes. Flashlights and rechargeable batteries are very important.

--Captain Paddy Timmons, USMC 2009 - 2014

And speaking of rechargeable batteries, Eneloop is the best brand. These batteries are far and away the best I have seen on the market. The numbers to look for are the number of re-chargings that the battery can take and the shelf-life before the no longer holds a charge. The latest version of Eneloops can be recharged 2100 times, and when they are five years old they will still hold 70% of their charge. In this respect, the numbers advertised by Eneloop are far higher than the equivalent numbers on other brands of rechargeable batteries, and it is not even close. So stock up on AA and AAA sizes of Eneloop batteries. They cost a little more than

Energizer or Duracell rechargeable batteries, but they are well-worth it.

One thing to keep in mind: battery life in rechargeable batteries is dependent on the temperature of the storage area. Make sure that you store your rechargeable batteries in as cool a location as possible. A battery stored in a hot area will not last as long.

As for recharging these batteries, if home electricity is still available, no problem. A lot of times Eneloop sells its batteries with a wall charger. If you cannot get a wall charger with your Eneloop batteries, go and buy a La Crosse battery charger. They are durable and do the best job charging batteries. Unlike other battery chargers, they independently charge each battery, and they shut off the charging when the battery is fully charged. La Crosse chargers charge both AA and AAA batteries, and these chargers cost a little more. The $30 base model is what I use and I am very happy with it.

My La Crosse charger also comes with a car adaptor, so you can charge rechargeable batteries in your car or by any 12-volt DC cigarette lighter-type charger. For truly off-the-grid or SHTF living, it would be a good idea to plug in one of these La Crosse battery chargers into to a cigarette lighter socket extension cord, and then on to a car battery that is itself recharged by solar panels. In fact, this is a future project of mine.

But it is possible to harness solar power to recharge these rechargeable batteries by an off-the-shelf system. While there are some other solar battery chargers out there on the market, the one that most impresses me is the Goal Zero solar battery charger. The solar panel is small and flexible, and meant to stretch across the back of a hiker's backpack. The solar panel then charges a separate battery-charger unit, which also has a USB port so that you can simultaneously charge up your Kindle or smart phone. All in all, a great unit, and it does not take forever to recharge your batteries.

Of these Goal Zero solar battery chargers are pricey, over $110 on Amazon. But however you do it, the flashlight is very important, and flashlights need constantly-recharged batteries to do the job. It is for this reason that I encourage everyone to stock up on high-lumen flashlights, Eneloop AA and AAA batteries, and rechargers, both Goal Zero and La Crosse. Nighttime illumination is one of the more important pillars in your preparations.

One last thing: steer clear of items that contain their own internal rechargeable battery, like wind-up flashlights or radios. These items might seem like a good deal but they aren't. The batteries in these items cannot be replaced and are not nearly as good as Eneloop batteries. Better to stay with flashlights and radios that use AA or AAA batteries, which can be replaced with other batteries when they run down.

Dorky-Looking Cars

If you're like me, you look forward to buying the biggest, baddest, meanest-looking prepper truck, lifted a few inches and painted camo or flat black. Even if you don't carry around a gun, you plan on putting a gun-rack in it just to look cool. The end result will be a chest-thumping, testosterone-oozing vehicle that will stick out and be the first thing taken away from you in case of a prolonged disaster where the rule of law has disappeared. Then you will be left to walk or hitch-hike everywhere.

Jim Rawles suggests buying a modest-looking, obviously run-down car that will not attract attention, and he is right. I would go a step further and suggest that as a prepper mobile, you buy one of the dorkiest-looking car from the 1960's or early 1970's.

A car from the 1960's or early 1970's does not have the smog and pollution control laws applied to it, so upkeep will cost very little. And in cars from these years, tuning up, changing oil and other maintenance jobs are very simple and easy.

If you are working with a group of people who will meet at a camp, consider getting the group to agree on the same car, like for example a 1970 Ford LTD, so that everyone could cannibalize car parts from each other if needed.

Also, a four-door, full-size car is best. If all else fails, you can sleep in it and pack a lot of your belongings in it and survive that way. A full-size car from the early 1970's could sleep four adults fairly comfortably, not including the trunk. And the trunks can carry suitcases-full of clothing and supplies.

Another priority would be stripped-down, lesser brands of the same type of car. Chevrolet instead of Cadillac, Ford instead of Lincoln or Mercury, and Dodge instead of Chrysler. That way, there will be fewer electronic gadgets that will break down and not be able to be repaired.

For example, compare the Chevrolet Impala from the early 1970's with the Cadillac Sedan DeVille from the same time period. Same chassis, but the Chevrolet has manual window openers and a regular trunk opener, while the Cadillac has electronic windows and some fancy-schmancy trunk-closer, so that all you need to do with the trunk is barely push it down and listen for a "click," after which the trunk-closer takes it from there and electronically closes the truck the final few inches. If spare parts were a problem, the owner of the Cadillac would not be able to operate the windows and trunk, while the Chevrolet owner would.

One of the things we preppers concern ourselves with is the possibility of an electro-magnetic pulse, or "EMP," which, whether from a rogue country exploding a nuke high in our atmosphere, or by the sun, called a "coronal mass ejection," or "CME," will fry most electronics. In fact, word has it that an EMP blast is a normal, accepted "first-strike" of a mass invasion, should it ever happen, from the United States military or any other country with the capability. A car with hardly any electronics in it, like cars from before 1967, will be more likely to run after an EMP or CME. Reportedly, the older the car is, the better the chances of the car surviving an EMP or a CME.

And lest you think this concern is silly, remember that there actually was a CME in 1859, which was called the "Carrington Event," and it fried what few electronics there were at the time. It has also been reported that in July, 2012, the Earth barely missed a solar flare that would have caused another CME. If the solar flare had occurred a week earlier than it did, Earth's electrical grid could have been fried and we would all still be trying to pick up the pieces even today.

So the mechanics of a car should be as simple as possible. The type of fuel a car uses is also a concern. Frankly, more than a few gallons of gas stored anywhere is a potential firebomb. Gasoline is explosive and flammable, and very dangerous to store. For this reason, cars with a diesel engine might be a good alternative. Diesel is not nearly as dangerous to store.

There is also a process whereby you can make your own diesel fuel, called biodiesel. The method is outside the scope of this book, but it is possible to buy equipment and raw materials to make diesel fuel out of vegetable or other oils. Sometimes the end result requires some slight modifications to your engine. I have seen advertisements of backyard biodiesel manufacturing plants that will produce usable biodiesel for as low as 30 cents a gallon!

As I wrote above, it should be a concern to get an unattractive car, or a car that a vigilante at a roadblock will not be tempted to steal from you. A hopped-up, 4x4 nice-looking pick-up truck would be the first thing some road-blockers would take from you at gunpoint. Meanwhile, a dorky-looking 1971 Dodge Polara or Buick Centurion, for example, or just about any AMC car from that time period (don't get me started on AMC cars and how ugly they were!), especially with some rust and uneven paint patterns, will be less-likely to be taken away.

Such a car could be in perfect mechanical condition, but if it looks dorky enough, it will be less likely to be taken from you. There are some other things you can do to make your car less likely to be taken away: uneven paint, like a door painted with gray primer, would make the car less attractive. Also, if your car has a front grill, remove it. Grills are only useful to deflect rocks at high speeds, which is not an issue in a long-tern collapse. A car with a missing grill will still drive fine and look ugly.

If the car has any hubcaps, remove them. That would be an easy and harmless way to make your car less attractive.

One last thing about the mechanics of a car from this time period: the body can look like junk, but if the car engine runs well, it serves the basic transportation purposes you need. One trick you can do to a gasoline-powered car from the 1960's or early 1970's is to temporarily remove a spark plug wire from the distributor cap. That way, the engine will still run fine but will sound bad. Anyone inclined to take a car away from someone at gunpoint would most likely move on to another car whose engine sounded better.

Regarding paint: if you are tempted to paint your prepper car real military camouflage, don't. That would only make the car more attractive to those who would take the car away. If you want to have the car a color that would blend in with your property and not be seen from outside, consider painting it with some store-bought camouflage spray paint. If camouflage is not available, paint the car with flat tan or green, depending on the surroundings of your property.

And finally, make sure that your exhaust is quiet. A quiet exhaust will enable you to drive around and attract much less attention.

Motorcycles

Having a lightweight motorcycle with dirt tires, also known as "dual sport," would also be a good idea. In my opinion, the engine displacement should be 350cc, or less. There are not so many motorcycles available from the 1960's and early 1970's, so in case of EMP or CME, you may be out of luck. The appearance of a motorcycle should be messed up so as to make it less attractive, but make sure to keep the exhaust in good shape. A motorcycle with a good exhaust system can go off-road and not attract too much attention, while a motorcycle with screwed-up exhaust will attract attention from miles away. I have also noticed that the older motorcycle, the higher up the exhaust pipe. So if you are giving a ride to someone, their leg is much more likely to be seriously burned with an older motorcycle.

A main advantage to a motorcycle is speed and agility, as a motorcyclist can quickly get to a location, and go around just about any obstruction. For motorcycles with engines smaller than 350cc, the gas mileage is at least 50, and sometimes as high as 80 miles per gallon. A "dual" motorcycle can travel off-road as well as on the highways. And, as has been shown in countless third world countries, as many as five people can grab and hold onto a motorcycle while it is going.

Of course, motorcycles are not perfect. Their agility makes the motorcycle less safe than a car. Unlike a car, if a motorcycle driver is shot at, there is not much between the bullet and the driver. Also, unlike a car, a motorcycle does not have the capability of carrying very much cargo.

There are ways around this. Motorcycles have the ability to use saddle bags, which can carry at least some cargo. Also, it is possible to make a trailer that would connect onto the back of a motorcycle. In order to do this you would probably need to start with a trailer that is made for an ATV, and weld an extension arm onto the back of the motorcycle, just above the license plate.

Paracord

This is one of those things that is great and cheap. Originally used in World War Two by parachuters, paracord has been found to be very useful in any number of situations by campers and military people alike.

"Paracord 550," as it is known, has been tested to support 550 pounds. You can break apart the paracord and find that there are several individual strings inside it, each of which can also be used.

Paracord can be used to do a lot of things. Here are a few examples: it can be used to support a tent between two trees, or as replacement shoe strings. Paracord can also be used as clothes line. In case of a large wound, paracord can be used as a tourniquet. When a pet loses a collar or leash, paracord can serve as a substitute. You can use paracord to suspend food up in a tree so that bears don't get at it. Paracord can also be used to make a hammock.

The smaller, internal strings of paracord can also be used as sewing thread, dental floss, and fishing line. In a pinch, one of the internal strings of paracord could be used to suture cuts and wounds.

I found 100 feet of paracord for sale on Amazon for $9, so there is no reason not to stock up on this stuff. And the paracord that you find on Amazon and Ebay is made in the USA.

If you look on Ebay, you can find many people making and selling different things with paracord. You can find belts, bracelets, key chains, knife handles and watchbands, all made out of paracord. The beautiful things about having a paracord bracelet, for example, is that if you need to hike home, and camp outdoors along the way, you can break apart the paracord and use it.

Paracord bracelets can be tucked around different things and they will not be in the way. I keep a paracord bracelet tied around my Sports Berkey Bottle. I also have a paracord bracelet on my emergency backpack, connecting stuff to the backpack, just like a lanyard.

So, while it is still cheap today, paracord is one of those things that will be extremely valuable in a SHTF situation.

Non-Gun Weapons

Have you ever seen the YouTube videos out there on what happened in the wake of Hurricane Katrina in New Orleans in 2005? Citizens, counting on protecting themselves with their guns, as if the Second Amendment guaranteed such things. Silly citizens, the right to bear arms is only guaranteed in theory!

But seriously, the Second Amendment is included in the United States Constitution for a reason, but apparently the powers-that-be never got the memo. Either that, or they choose to ignore that right whenever there is an opportunity.

Really, if you go to YouTube and search for videos having to do with Katrina and guns, you will be astounded when you see police officers and national guardsmen going from door to door, confiscating firearms from law-abiding people. People who were at home, doing nothing wrong. Sure, there was some looting after the hurricane, but weapons were being confiscated from people under the theory that the gun-owners *might* use their weapons illegally.

There was one elderly lady, Patricia Konie, who was being interviewed by the press *a week after* the hurricane, when police unexpectedly came to her house. In full view of the cameras that were rolling, the police ordered her to leave her house, and when they saw that she had a small revolver, they rushed her, grabbed the gun, punched her in the face and slammed her to the ground. Among other injuries, Ms. Konie got a fractured shoulder. She was arrested, held in jail for a few hours before being released with no charges filed. "I thought they were going to kill me," she later said.

What had this woman done wrong? She was inside her house when a disaster happened nearby. That's it! The authorities used that as an excuse to enter her house without any warrant (that would have been a hassle, don't you know), and demand any gun that she might have used to defend herself with.

This is known as "excessive rule of law," or EROL, and the possibility exists for this to happen in each and every case of any prolonged disaster or SHTF situation. In any future disaster, it would be naïve not to think that the same thing could not happen all over again. I can see the rhetoric now: for the "public safety," guns have to be taken away from "potential criminals" who have "no need" to possess "dangerous weapons like these." And if the gun has a certain look about it, or is solid black, it may be considered an "assault weapon." The government, or what is left of it, would best be able to protect us all if only they had a monopoly on gun possession. For our own good, of course.

It is for this reason that I suggest you buy and stockpile non-gun weapons, and as many as possible. Specifically, axes, machetes, knives, crowbars, bows and arrows, crossbows, hatchets, and whatever else you can use to protect yourself if guns are declared illegal. Pepper spray, and hornet and wasp spray also work. Anyone who envisions protecting themselves and their family using only their guns is living in fantasyland.

Specifically, machetes are very useful, not only for protection but for other purposes as well. In other countries, machetes are seen as extremely useful non-gun weapons, as my friend Paul Hammond recently wrote me:

> Cal, you should really write about the importance of non-gun defensive weapons, especially if times get really bad and the government takes everyone's guns away. As we all know, in extreme times, the government may exhibit "excessive rule of law," or EROL. By this I mean guns may either be taken by force, or in exchange for necessary items like food and/or drinking water. Should there be a prolonged national emergency, food and drinking water will become vital, more so than guns. If we should ever find ourselves in this situation I believe the best multipurpose

weapon we can arm ourselves with would be the machete. Hear me out on this.

As an American I've spent years living abroad in several developing counties. And I can tell you that in countries from Jamaica, to Guatemala, to Nicaragua, the machete is the tool of choice. This multipurpose tool is very light-weight, can be sheathed for easy carrying, holds an edge for a very long time, and can be made razor sharp with nothing more than a sharpening stone, and five minutes work. I've seen Jamaican bushmen fell a 4" diameter tree in less than a minute, and then shave part of that tree down for kindling. While somewhat larger than a bowie knife you can still filet a fish, protect yourself against snakes, take down enough vegetation to make a shelter, and open a coconut (which is essential in this part of the world when no drinking water can be found).

Among all of the useful tasks the machete is good for, it's also an ideal weapon for self-defense. I have had a gun, in the United States, and a machete, in Jamaica, brandished at me. I can assure you, the thought of being hit with that machete is a thousand times more terrifying than being shot at. At least with a gun there's the chance of the shooter missing me, the gun jamming, or a shot that misses vital organs. Even if you're hit non-lethally with a machete, you're still going to be out of commission for quite a while. It would be very ugly.

Cal, I urge you and all of the other preppers out there, not to overlook the machete as a tool that needs to be added to your supplies. I have seen first-hand what can be done with them, and I now have my machete next to my bed at all times, just in case.

--Paul Hammond

So there you have it: guns are important, and possessing them is our right as United States citizens, but it would only be prudent to stockpile non-gun weapons, including machetes. Knives, crowbars, bows and arrows, crossbows, and hatchets would also be good to have. I just took a peek on Amazon, and a Gerber, 25-inch long machete, complete with sheath, sells for only $13. The back side of the blade is a wood saw, so you can also use it to saw wood.

And keeping any blade sharp is also important. For this, I like the compact Smith's Pocket Knife Sharpener, which sells for $9 on Amazon.

I also noticed that Amazon sells an 18-inch crowbar, which for some reason is called a "wrecking bar," made by Tekton, for $8. In an SHTF situation, these items will be extremely valuable. Besides defending yourself, crowbars can be used to get inside abandoned buildings.

One last thing on this subject: watch for sales of shovels, axes and pick-axes at hardware stores. Make it a habit. Every time you are in a hardware store, before you leave, walk through the aisle of shovels and watch for sales of these items. If you can get a shovel for less than $7, grab it, and add it to your collection of shovels.

At our house, because we live in the country, we try to have round-head shovels all around the house, just leaning against the side of the house. That way, if any of my family comes across a poisonous snake, we can quickly reach for a shovel to kill the snake. And who knows, if a mountain lion wants to attack us (this has never happened yet but a mountain lion killed a neighbor's lamb), a shovel would be pretty good protection and certainly better than nothing. Also, there is that part of the book of Revelation (Rev 6:8) that discusses people in the end-times being killed by wild beasts of the earth. I would rather be prepared against stuff like that.

Of course, you can always use a shovel for, you know, actual digging.

Same for axes. Depending on the disaster, there may be no more gasoline or machines that can be used to chop wood to keep yourself warm in the winter. For that reason you should have several axes handy.

And speaking of using shovels to defend yourself with, there is a great folding shovel that has a blade on the side of it. Gerber makes one of these and it sells for about $42 on Amazon. It is a great shovel and the weight and handle are just right to use the blade on the side of it for self-defense. I bought a black nylon holder for mine, so I can fold up the shovel and insert it into the nylon holder, which can be attached to my bug-out bag.

But you should stockpile all of this stuff. You might find yourself among a group of people, or your family, at a bug-out location, and you will need those people to be armed, or non-gun armed, as well. Non-gun weaponry should be everyone's "Plan B" for self-defense.

Dutch Ovens

I'm not sure if these things are originally from Holland, or if their name comes from two people who bought the first one and split the cost, you know, as in *going Dutch*, but these things are great!

A Dutch oven is basically a big, cast-iron pot that you can nestle right in the middle of a fire and cook your meal by the ambient heat or coals of the fire around it. The lids are even made with putting coals on top of the lid in mind. In a camping situation, this is as close to a hot oven as you will ever get.

Every prepper should get to know the Dutch oven. In case of a longer-term collapse, or a true SHTF situation, every meal you have could be cooked in one of these. And I mean, every meal.

The only catch to Dutch ovens, is not so much a catch as it is a feature: so-called "seasoning." In seasoning a Dutch oven, you are supposed to smear the surface of a Dutch oven with oil, bacon fat or lard and cook it at 350 degrees in a regular oven for an hour. This is pretty messy, and makes a lot of smoke in the house. And after cooking in the Dutch oven, you can use warm water but you aren't supposed to use soap, as soap may take away the seasoning in the cast iron.

Dutch ovens, made by Lodge, usually sell for about $65 apiece at Walmart. We bought one, seasoned it, and started using it immediately. You don't need to only use it only in a campfire, so we used it on our stove first, then in the oven.

We made some great beef stew. First, we browned some stew beef in the Dutch oven on the stove. Then we added a can of whole corn, with the water from the can, a cut-up onion, a small bag of pre-cut carrots, two cut potatoes, and a can of green beans. We then seasoned it all, and then cooked it in the oven at 350 degrees for ninety minutes. We added salt and pepper to taste. The result was a great beef stew that tasted like it was made from an ancient family recipe! It was so good, even the left-overs for this stew were gobbled up by someone in our house the next day!

Here are a couple of other Dutch oven recipes I have used:

Road Kill Chili:

Ingredients:

2 pounds of ground beef
1 minced onion
1 clove of minced garlic
12 ounces of diced tomatoes
1 bay leaf
3 jalapeno peppers finely minced, without the seeds and ribs
12 ounces of V8 Juice
2 teaspoons of salt
2 teaspoons of lemon pepper
2 teaspoons of black pepper
2 teaspoons of chili powder
1 teaspoon of cumin

Instructions:

Cook down the ground beef, onion, garlic, and salt
Drain fat. Add V8, bay leaf, tomatoes, pepper, chili powder and cumin.

Cook covered for 2 1/2 hours, stirring every half hour

Remove bay leaf and serve.

Ojai Breakfast

Ingredients:

1 medium onion, diced
16 eggs
1 pound of bacon, chopped
1 small chopped potato
2 cups of shredded cheese (cheddar preferred)
salt and pepper to taste
cayenne pepper to taste

Instructions:

Brown the chopped bacon with heat underneath only, without the lid. Stir occasionally, and before the bacon is completely done, add the onion and sauté in the bacon juices until the onion begins to be translucent. Add the eggs and potato. Scramble, and then slowly fold over the egg mixture until it is set at the desired firmness. Add salt, pepper, cayenne pepper to taste. Remove from heat, sprinkle on cheese. Serve.

Honey Bees

Store sugar! When you try to survive cooking your own food outdoors, or in a grid-down situation, it is very handy to have something to mix with your food that sweetens it. If you buy it in bulk, sugar is fairly cheap. And sugar has an extremely-long shelf-life, so long as it is kept in a cool, dark and dry place.

But have you ever thought of keeping honey bees? Honey is a renewable resource, meaning that it is something whose supply can be regenerated every few months. Once you have finished off your last supply of honey, go to the bees and steal a new supply of honey. Unless you have a sugarcane plantation nearby, you cannot replenish your supply of sugar like you can with honey.

First, the bees themselves are good to have around. They help your plants pollinate like crazy. I remember when my wife disregarded my advice and got our first beehive, we had this white rose bush near our back patio door. It was growing in a raised bed that was haphazardly made of rocks and concrete. Within a year, the rose bush had grown so big that the rose bush was literally getting too big for the raised bed! Really – rocks were getting pushed out of the bed wall and the concrete of the raised bed was starting to crack! The raised bad had to be rebuilt because of the bees!

Pollination from bees helps plants grow. Also, this is why you notice the white boxes of beehives every time you drive by a farm.

And don't confuse bees with hornets, yellow jackets or wasps. Whenever a flying insect stings, everyone usually assumes it is a bee, which is sometimes possible. But hornets, yellow jackets and wasps have stingers that can be used to sting all the time, whereas a bee stinger can be used only once. After using its stinger, a bee dies. So bees are choosier when they decide whom and when to sting.

Bees are much more concerned with collecting nectar that is made into honey for the hive. And because the honey bees collect nectar at the same time they collect pollen, honey helps your body deal with allergies. In my experience, this is not a sudden thing. If you are suffering from allergies, you won't notice any immediate relief from eating honey. Rather, it is a longer-term proposition.

Many years ago, after I moved to the country, the first spring was a killer. I had never experienced itchy eyes and a sore throat like that! I heard about honey and allergies, so within the next few months I made sure to eat some local honey at least once a week. A lot of times, I would pour some honey into my morning coffee. And the next spring, my allergies were mostly kept in check. It works!

But make sure to get local honey, not commercialized honey from far away. Some "honey" on the market nowadays is really a sweet gel that is called honey but does not really resemble true honey. And even if you find honey from a faraway location, it will not help your allergies because they are specific to your location. Make sure that the honey you buy is from your immediate area, or at least from a nearby county.

Honey is also a natural antibacterial that can be applied to cuts and burns to help in healing. The next time you get a minor cut, instead of antibacterial cream, try putting on some honey before you put on a band aid. You will notice the cut heals faster.

I have also heard stories of people with severe diabetes, whose toes or limbs are rotting off from lack of circulation, and they have applied honey to stop the gangrene from spreading.

Also, in harvesting the honey, you will be able to also harvest wax that can be used to make candles. In a grid-down situation, anything that can help with illumination is very important.

Wax from beehives can also be used to coat and preserve cheese. In a situation where there is no refrigeration, that would be handy.

Honey and wax can both be used as items for barter. A few months ago, I bought 24 8-ounce plastic honey containers to hold some honey that we harvested from our bees. I felt the $26 I paid was a bit steep, but as we bottled the honey and stored it away, I knew this would be used for barter someday. An 8-ounce container is small, but not too small. It kind of felt like money in the bank.

And honey has an eternal shelf-life. It never spoils! Reportedly, numerous explorers have found jars of honey or honeycomb that contained honey in the tombs of the ancient Egyptian kings. And despite the passage of several millennia between this honey's collection and discovery, it was still good to eat! So keep that in mind: honey will last in storage. Even if it crystalizes, you can just warm it up and eat it like always.

As I have mentioned elsewhere in this book, morale should be an important concern in your preps. And if you are a person who appreciates some alcohol to drink, note that honey can be mixed in warm water and yeast, and fermented into a kind of wine called "mead." I have had some, and mead would not be my first choice with some nice brie and crackers, but it is still enjoyable. If you want to try this before making it, go to a wine store and ask for it. Mead is mass-produced and sold for about the same price of wine.

One last thing about honey, and this is not something I have yet tried, but it sounds I interesting: honey bee hives can be used as defense. The idea sounds intriguing. Suppose there is an opening to your property that would like to keep trespasser-free. You could set up a couple of bee hive boxes there and the normally-observant person would see a lot of bees flying around and stay clear of that area. You could even leave out some bowls of sugary water to make sure the bees stay there.

So make honey bee hives and the collection of honey and wax as part of your preps. While there is some up-front cost, it is regenerating and cheap!

Although I was underwhelmed with the size and cost of this jar (a little over a dollar apiece), this small 8-ounce size jar full of honey is great for stockpiling.

Fish Antibiotics

Mark this one in the "while it lasts" category, because there is no way this will last for a long time. I am no doctor or pharmacist, and I have pretty neat handwriting, which certifies my total disconnect from the medical profession. But you don't have to take my word for it. I have seen many YouTube videos and blog sites that show how some of the antibiotics that are sold for use in fish aquariums are exactly the same as the antibiotics that are proscribed to humans. One YouTube video I saw even had Dr. Bones, also known as Dr. Joe Alton, compare the actual pills given to fish and to humans, and the manufacturer name and code numbers on the pills matched up identically. Like I said, there is no way this will last long before the government steps in and makes it illegal.

Antibiotics can be used to treat all sorts of maladies: strep throat, urinary tract infection, kidney infections, urinary tract infections, diarrhea, anthrax, pneumonia, and bronchitis, just to name a few. Notice these are all bacterial infections. For viruses, like the common cold or flu, antibiotics do not do a thing.

When you shop for these antibiotics, you will notice the names are not what you expect. "Fish Pen" and "Fish Pen Forte" are really Penicillin, and "Fish Flox" and "Fish Flox Forte" are really Ciprofloxacin. (By the way, Cipro is good to have on hand in case the Anthrax terrorist from 2001 makes a re-appearance.) As with regular human antibiotics, the tablets all have different sizes, from 100 mg to 500 mg dosages.

Nurse Amy and Doctor Bones, at the website doomandbloom.net, have a great evaluation of fish antibiotics. You should do your own research on fish antibiotics, not only the types of antibiotics you can get, but what dosage pill you should use to address which ailments. This stuff can get complicated.

You should also educate yourself on the problems caused by their misuse of antibiotics. This is why these pills are normally as regulated as they are. Some people are allergic to various antibiotics, and some of these pills are not safe for children or pregnant women. Also taking too many antibiotics can cause the development of resistant bacteria, so that taking antibiotics in the future will do no good at all. Also, the overuse or misuse of antibiotics can cause the onset of an unusual and potentially fatal form of diarrhea, known as c.diff.

In conclusion, antibiotics either prescribed by a regular doctor or fish antibiotics should be taken very rarely, and only when they are legitimately needed.

But having antibiotics is better than not having them, especially in a prolonged SHTF situation. A few years ago, the History Channel aired a movie named *After Armageddon*, in which one of the main characters survived all the end-times problems that were thrown his way, only to (spoiler alert!) die from a relatively minor blood infection. The point was clearly made that he would have survived if he had any antibiotics to take. But the character, like everyone nowadays, never thought to stockpile antibiotics.

So do yourself a favor and seriously look into, study, and stockpile fish antibiotics. In a true SHTF situation, there will be no doctor to advise on and prescribe this stuff. A good website to start is at Fishmoxfishflex.com. Campingsurvival.com also has some fish antibiotics. As with a lot of important stuff to stockpile, prescription antibiotics should be stored in a cool, dark place to prolong their shelf life.

Board Games And Entertainment

I really detest board games -- I just cannot stand them! As my family can attest, when I am forced to join a group in a board game, I lose on purpose, thereby increasing the chance that I will be left alone the next time a big group is tempted to get together and play a board game.

But things are different in a true SHTF-situation. If you are part of a group of people who retreat to the hills or a common bug-out situation, when you are not making sure that there is food to eat and water to drink or the location is secure, or other needs taken care of, time might drag. You and your group will need something to do to pass the time and keep yourselves occupied. And let's face it: you will be on a slippery slope of anxiety and depression. Good morale will be a very important consideration, and some distractions may make a big difference.

The good news, at least for me, is that you need not play any board games that you accumulate for your retreat location. Just go to a local Salvation Army, Goodwill, or a garage sale, a pick up a few board games. The only looking inside you will need to do is to make sure all the parts of the game are there.

And that brings me to another consideration: avoid games with many parts, or paper money (like Monopoly), and games that require an excessive amount of writing down, or score-keeping. Any game that will become unplayable if it misses a single part will not do you any good.

Chess and checkers are OK, as everyone seems to know the rules and parts can be easily replaced as they get lost. Rocks and bottle caps can be used as games pieces if the need arises.

Playing cards are useful in providing distractions, and they are cheap. I just saw 12 sets of playing cards for sale on Amazon for $7.

With a standard deck of cards, you can play Crazy Eights with up to six people, or as few as two. This is an easy, fast-paced game that can be played for hours, or even in tournament structure. Points can be tallied over hours, days, or even weeks. Poker is also fun. Then, there is always Solitaire, if no one else wants to play.

I once played a tolerable game of Uno with a few people. Uno has its own set of cards. There are a couple of variations of playing Uno using only one deck; so a good Uno deck, or maybe two, can be valuable.

Having on hand a bunch of dice is also a good idea for entertainment. Pig, High Dice, Yahtzee, Farkle, Craps, are all relatively fun games that can be played only with dice, and maybe an honest person keeping score.

And, of course charades is a game that can be played with no equipment at all!

Musical instruments might also help pass the time, assuming you have a lot of room so that you don't need to hear a bad player. Harmonicas, accordions, trumpets, flutes, recorders, and ukuleles and guitars, so long as you have extra strings.

Novels will also help pass the time, and the average Salvation Army and Goodwill have a ton of old paperbacks for very little money. And remember, you don't need to read them, you only need to make sure they aren't smut, then buy them and load them at your retreat location somewhere.

Some people might accumulate lots of books on their Kindles or ebooks, and that might work for shorter-term disasters. But keep in mind that with a long-term disaster or a true SHTF situation, those e-books will run out of electricity. So they will become useless unless you have a way to recharge them.

Female Stuff

I'm just a guy, so discussing or even advising on this subject is not only new, but kind of uncomfortable for me. But I will give it a try. Bear with me.

While tampons in some form have been made and used by menstruating women for thousands of years, the idea of buying a mass-produced tampon and using it when that time of the month came around is relatively new in human history. Only a couple generations ago, when that time of the month came around, most women would fold rags and place them snugly in their groin area, so as to soak up any menstrual blood that was emitted. That is where the expression "on the rag" came from. It might have been a little cumbersome, but by and large it worked.

For a family or group who has or will include in its ranks a woman who is of menstruating age, the immediate goal might be to stock up on as many tampons as you can buy. And in the case of a shorter-term disaster, that will work fine. But keep in mind that the tampons used can only be used once, and for a woman going through her period, that could mean using several tampons in any given day. A professor at New York University recently estimated that the average American women uses over 11,000 tampons in her lifetime.

And in case you are wondering, trying to clean and reuse a tampon is very unsafe, so don't even think about it.

Another option is to stock up on sanitary pads. These have a dual purpose, as they can be used for female issues, but also as a bandage to treat a wound. If any cut is large enough, it will need pressure on it from a sanitary object that soaks up blood, so sanitary napkins are great for menstrual as well as wound-care uses. Stocking up on them would be a good idea for these two purposes, and the Dollar Store has been the source of my stockpile of these things.

But what about a longer-term disaster, or a true societal collapse? In time, any given stockpile of tampons or sanitary napkins would run out, leaving the woman in question to use the "rag" method of old, where she would need to make sure to clean and dry the rags so that they can be reused over and over.

There is another answer, and it is a recent development: the "menstrual cup." I will not try to go into too much detail here, but it is basically a plastic, reusable tampon that can be cleaned and reused. According to women who have used it, while it takes some practice to get it to work right, it has really improved their lives. Some women are so happy with these menstrual cups, they think of it as a widely-kept secret.

These things are generally made of safe, BPA-, dioxin- and latex-free plastic that is non-allergenic for most women. Menstrual cups last for years, and they come in two different sizes, depending on whether the woman using them has given birth or not. So when stocking up on them, it would be a good idea to accumulate some for both sizes.

The bad news: these things aren't cheap. I just checked on some for sale on Amazon, and for the menstrual cups I looked at, they cost $30 for two. I can imagine that stocking up a whole bucket-full of these things would cost a lot of money.

On the other hand, this might be one of those items that for a large prepper group would be very valuable. Women would be freed up from having to work with rags at that time of the month, and able to do other things for the group.

Cayenne Pepper

One of the spices that is great to stockpile is cayenne pepper. This is an important spice, and very cheap. Small containers of cayenne pepper can be found at the Dollar Store.

Cayenne pepper helps with circulation, and cayenne pepper mixed with hot water has been known to help with heart attacks. (In fact, aspirin is another good thing to give to someone at the onset of a heart attack.)

Cayenne pepper is also good to have around for wound care. Take a palmful of cayenne pepper and apply it directly to the cut or wound. Not only will cayenne pepper quickly slow or stop the flow of blood from the wound, it will also disinfect the wound. Cayenne pepper has both anti-fungal and anti-bacterial properties.

For larger wounds that bleed more, nosebleeds, or for internal bleeding like stomach ulcers, the patient should drink a teaspoon of cayenne pepper mixed into a glass of warm water. Reportedly, the bleeding will stop in less than a minute! Cayenne has a way or equalizing blood pressure on both sides of the bleeding, thus causing the blood to clot pretty quickly.

Cayenne pepper is also a tasty spice -- great to add to food. Recently in our household we have begun adding cayenne pepper to our morning eggs. It also adds a nice taste to chili. I have also heard stories of people carrying a bottle of cayenne pepper with them when they go to eat at a Mexican food restaurant. If the food that arrives at the table lacks enough kick, they add the cayenne pepper to the food.

Like I wrote above, cayenne pepper is available at the Dollar Store, and it is not too expensive elsewhere.

Another great thing about cayenne pepper, and in all peppers in general, is that you can grow it in your garden and there is less of a chance that a rabbit or deer will come by and eat it. The plant is too hot for those animals to eat and enjoy. They will move on to your potatoes or tomatoes instead.

Electrolyte Recipes

My pastor has a story in which he spent a week on a mission trip in Cambodia, repeatedly sweating and drinking water, and then he returned home. The night after he got home, his wife overheard him talking complete gibberish, and then he passed out. He woke up in the hospital, and was informed that his body, while being rehydrated from all the water he had drunk on his trip, had become depleted of electrolytes. In the hospital he was fed a lot of electrolyte replacement drinks, kind of Gatorade but much more intense. He eventually recovered but today he is a big advocate of drinking Gatorade and the like whenever he or people around him work in the sun and sweat.

This story matches the story of how Gatorade got its start back in the 1960's. Back then, an assistant coach and a medical doctor, both employed by the University of Florida sports department, recognized that the players for the Florida Gators football team were feeling weak, "wilting," as they put it, and in some cases fainting during football practices in the hot, Florida sun. After some brainstorming, they put together a water-based drink with added sodium, potassium and carbohydrates – the exact minerals that the body sweats during physical exertion. These are known as "electrolytes," those minerals that regulate the body's nerve and muscle function, maintain blood pressure and pH, and help rebuild damaged tissue. The result was the early version of the Gatorade sports drink. In the next several years, the Florida Gators football team greatly improved its win-loss record, and word spread. Eventually, most sports teams feature Gatorade sports drink on its sidelines.

The idea that water was not enough to replenish the body after a lot of sweating was a real breakthrough! Gatorade, and its main competitor, Powerade, are good, but I have found an electrolyte replacement drink that I prefer, and it is called Sqwincher. Sqwincher places a high priority on going "sugar free," which in my opinion is a non-issue, but I still like it. It is fashionable to sneer at all of these drinks, but they do the job of replenishing what the body sweats out after some heat and real physical exertion.

Gatorade and Powerade can be bought premixed in bottles. Both Gatorade and Sqwincher come in powder forms, which you can pour into a bottle of water, shake the bottle a few times, and drink. They both have several flavors. For me, the lemonade flavor of Sqwincher is the best.

But what is a prepper to do? Especially a prepper trying to maximize his and her dollar in storing preps that matter? These powders are pretty expensive.

Homemade electrolyte drinks are the answer. You can store up ingredients to make electrolyte replacements drinks, and this will last a lot longer than Gatorade or Sqwincher powders. And who knows? This could be one of those preps that will be like another athlete's foot or jock itch cream, desperately needed by thousands of people in a true SHTF-setting, who never anticipated the need for this stuff.

The basic idea is to start with water, and mix in some fruit juice, the fresher the better. Even a watered-down fruit drink works. Then add salt, potassium, and some baking soda. The best source of potassium that I have found is "No-Salt," the salt substitute, or Morton Salt Substitute. (In my humble opinion, these salt-substitutes were designed to make us all appreciate the real taste of regular salt.) Bananas are also good for potassium.

While there are some exact recipes for these drinks that I have found, the easy way to make one of these drinks it to just add a "pinch" each of salt, potassium and baking soda to a fruit drink. Adding some fruit juice is also important.

In the recipes that I have found, honey seems to be a good added ingredient, and coconut water has been acclaimed by just about everyone who has seriously studied electrolytes. I hesitated including this in this book, because it might be a situation that rarely arises: but if you are ever in a setting where there are coconuts, try to get your hands on coconut water. Coconut water has been written up as the number one best, natural electrolyte replacement liquid out there. Coconut water has even been called "Nature's Gatorade." Even a splash of coconut water into your electrolyte replacement cocktail would make it immensely better.

Here are a few recipes of electrolyte replacements drinks that I have found:

4 cups of fresh water
1/4 cup of freshly squeezed lime juice
1/4 cup freshly squeezed lemon juice
(Or substitute ½ cup of orange juice)
1/8 teaspoon of salt
2 tablespoons natural sugar or honey

½ gallon of water
½ teaspoon of baking soda
2 tablespoons of agave nectar
½ tablespoon of sea salt

1 quart of water
2 tablespoons of sugar
½ teaspoon of baking soda
½ teaspoon of table salt
¼ teaspoon of salt substitute

2 quarts water
1 package of unsweetened Kool-aid, any flavor
1/2 cup sugar
1/2 tsp. salt
1/2 cup orange juice

Here are some ingredients to a homemade electrolyte-
replacement drink. Start with water, then add fruit juice,
baking soda, potassium (salt substitute), salt and honey.
You can use the banana as a chaser.

Bleach/Pool Shock

Bleach has many uses. Three main uses of bleach are: disinfecting water, disinfecting surfaces, and killing viruses. (Although boiling water for a minute or more, or filtering the water is the preferred way to disinfect water.)

The anti-viral uses of bleach were recently in the news. The Ebola scare from 2014, has mostly receded from the headlines, but if you remember that time period, the idiocy and political correctness of the government officials in charge was especially nerve-racking. It was rare to get a straight answer as to how this strain of Ebola would transmit from one person to another. And while other countries had no problem in closing their borders to people from Ebola-infected areas, the borders of the United States remained wide open for anyone from West Africa to fly in at their convenience. And of course, in a few cases, that is what happened. If you think about it, it is amazing that the Ebola scare of 2014 didn't become a full-fledged pandemic. It could have gotten extremely ugly.

With the same idiots still in charge of keeping us safe from Ebola, the even-worse Marburg virus, or who-knows-what-else could come our way, we preppers need to keep some bleach or bleach-making ingredients on hand to kill any deadly viruses that may come our way.

Unfortunately, bleach has a pretty short shelf life. Bleach starts to degrade after six months and after five years, it is little more than salty water. After five years, I certainly would not recommend you taste it or anything, but it is no longer useful as bleach.

Even worse, the manufacturers plan on the bleach they sell you degrading. They figure the product will take about six months to get the bleach from their factory to your store, and that you will immediately buy the bleach when it arrives at the store. If you happen to get some bleach that was at the back of the bleach selection for months, you might have bought some bleach that is already degraded before you even bring it to your house!

That is where pool shock comes in. Pool shock can be bought and stored, so that it can be mixed into water to produce bleach. That's right! You can store the ingredients to make your own bleach right at home. And the shelf-life of pool shock is at least ten years.

First, some safeguards. Pool shock powder is really intense. You should have a healthy fear in handling this stuff. Read and take seriously the handling and storage precautions listed on the containers that hold pool shock. Those packages have some pretty scary admonitions. Do not breathe pool shock dust, and make sure that you wear glasses when you handle it. Gloves are also a good idea when handling pool shock. And when you mix pool shock, make sure to you are in an open area, preferably with a slight wind blowing. Pool shock also needs to be stored in an area away from the direct sunlight, and in a cool, well-ventilated, dry area. Pool shock is very corrosive, so it needs to be well-diluted before coming in contact with anything.

Never add water to pool shock – only add small amounts of pool shock to water. Whenever you open the pool shock container, make sure it is pointed away from your face. This also applies to bleach.

And, whether it is pool shock or bleach, don't mix either with stuff like vinegar, ammonia or cleansers or water treatment products. That could create a toxic gas and the mixture could explode. Only mix pool shock with water.

It is also important to make sure that any spray or squirt bottles that you intend to use are empty and cleaned out before you put bleach in them. If the container has anything still in it that reacts with bleach, it could create a toxic gas and the mixture could explode.

I have found pool shock for sale at hardware stores, pool supply stores, and online at Amazon. Make sure the powder has at least

60% calcium-hypochlorite, not the "sodium" variety of pool shock. The other ingredients are usually listed at "other ingredients," which makes it easy. Also, make sure the pool shock you buy has no algaecides or fungicides in it.

Once you have the pool shock, you can make regular chlorine bleach, like what you would buy in the store, by mixing 2 tablespoons of pool shock with 3 cups of water. After you mix this, wait a few hours to let some inert ingredients settle. Then, separate the light-green liquid from the settled powder at the bottom. The light-green liquid is regular chlorine bleach. The powder that settled at the bottom should be discarded away from food and animals, as it is unsafe.

Of course, now that you have standard, household-strength bleach, the shelf-life issues apply. This bleach, just like the bleach you bought at the store, start to degrade pretty quickly.

Bleach that is diluted with water is the best disinfectant. A 10% bleach to 90% water mixture is the best, so dilute it again.

To disinfect drinking water, add eight drops of regular chlorine bleach to each gallon of water and keep it sealed. This will keep the water disinfected for a year. That rule is easy to remember: each gallon of water weighs eight pounds, and you put eight drops of chlorine bleach into each gallon to disinfect it. Kind of a "Rule of Eight."

Toilet Replacements

"We have a butt-washer in our hotel room!" I proudly announced in a letter home from my first trip to Europe. And it was true that we did indeed have a, uh, rear end washer in our hotel room. In fact, they are all over Europe. Everywhere we went! You would think that the rear ends all over Europe would be very clean.

Probably the main advantage to using a bidet is that you don't need to use toilet paper. And in a disaster situation or total SHTF, toilet paper will be rare or non-existent. Even those who stock up on pallets-full of toilet paper will eventually run out, if the disaster lasts long enough.

But there is a solution. Travel bidets are sold on Amazon for $10 to $15. I have used one, and while I will spare you the details, it is kind of gross but it works OK. It is pretty important to use lukewarm water to use in it, and allow the area down there to air-dry after you use the bidet.

I can also imagine in a disaster situation that hemorrhoid issues may be prevalent, and the travel bidet is a pretty gentle way to clean your rear end. These things would be excellent to stock up on, because in a real long-term SHTF situation, very few people out there will have toilet paper or anything close to it. A barter for a travel bidet would probably get something seriously expensive in exchange.

Admittedly, I dread the possibility of using the next toilet paper substitute, old Yellow Page books. Those pages in the books are made up of pretty thin paper, and in a disaster or SHTF situation, these pages could be torn out of the book, crumpled up a little to make them softer, and used for toilet paper. This alternative might be advisable for hard-core survivalists only, as the idea sounds pretty rough on the rear end. But it may be better than nothing, and Yellow Page books are given away for free anyway. Instead of throwing away your old Yellow Pages, you might as well keep them and store them somewhere.

Anyone who has had toddler kids knows the idea of rewashing diapers. Well, there is a prepper approach to going to the restroom that involves a similar idea: red shop towels. These things are cheap (Amazon sells 10 of them for $5), and can be used as substitute toilet paper. Then they must be washed and dried, which is pretty gross, but then they can be used again. Kind of like diapers. I would suggest a rule for your retreat location: everyone immediately washes the shop towels that they wiped with, and as soon as possible. Otherwise, the gross-ness is compounded, and disease may spread.

As for the actual toilets involved for someone outside of their home, I have several suggestions.

Composting toilets are a great way to have your toilet "off the grid," meaning that there is very little water hooked up to the toilet (or poured in by hand) and the toilet still disposes of what is put into it. It is possible to have the composting part of the toilet run by solar power or batteries. SanMar and Envirolet are two of the brands of composting toilets.

However there are many communities that do not allow composting toilets. And they aren't cheap: up to $2,000 is about normal. They also require work to hook up, vent, power up and empty when they are full. You will definitely miss your "flush it and forget it" toilet from the pre-SHTF days.

Here is a cheap version of the composting toilet: five-gallon buckets, about a quarter-full of sawdust, kitty litter, crunched up leaves, and/or some baking soda thrown in to further stop the smell. Add one of those pool floaties, also known as "noodles," sliced lengthwise in half, but not all the way through and put around the bucket's edge. That way it is not so uncomfortable to sit on one of these buckets and do your business. The entire set-up is so cheap that each family member can have their own. The more baking soda and sawdust, the less the smell.

Instead of the pool noodle floatie, you can always buy a "Tote-able Toilet Seat and Lid" from Emergency Essentials for $15 each. These come with a lid, which will keep the smell down in between emptying out this toilet.

Amazon also sells self-contained toilets, for prices of $40 to $130. They are usually marketed to campers, and they have a comfortable rim to sit on, and a separate container for the liquid that you flush into it. Some come with a specialized deodorant. When separate container fills up, you empty it somewhere and start over.

One cautionary note when it comes to sewage: I once saw a *Doomsday Prepper* show, in which someone had an outdoor toilet and, after somehow treating the contents of the toilet, they spread what was left in their garden as fertilizer. Be careful! Having raw sewage nearby a garden is dangerous. Even if there is a system you have whereby the sewage is treated, things can go wrong. People can also forget how to treat the sewage right, or even whether to treat it at all. In my opinion, it is best to just plan on just burying the sewage that is in one of these five-gallon buckets, and don't even think about digging it back up and using for compost for at least a year.

But you should take seriously the idea of "preparing for pooping." This is one of those issues that is totally ignored by almost all preppers out there.

Here is an example of my "prepper pooper" toilet. Doesn't it look inviting? OK seriously, it is better than nothing in a truly long-term disaster situation. The unit cost of this one was about $8. That "noodle" floatie thingy that you sit on can be removed so that it doesn't come in contact with the contents that you pour out.

Soap And Shampoo

There is no reason not to stock up on soap and shampoo. Walmart sells Ivory soap for only $3 for 10 bars, making the unit price of these bars of soap to be only 30 cents! Also, Walmart sells Suave shampoo for less than a dollar a bottle.

Washing your hands and hair is not only a hygienic issue, but it is also a morale issue. The few times in my life that I have gone for an extended period of time without bathing, I have felt pretty dirty and my mood declines. And, as I noted in the introduction of this book, morale is a huge fudge factor that effects how long you can survive without food, water, shelter, etc. So being clean could better enable you to survive an extended disaster.

And because soap and shampoo are to be used externally, the shelf life of these has to be pretty high. So it would be a good idea – and cheap -- to fill some 5-gallon buckets of shampoo and Ivory soap. If there is an extended disaster that requires you to go to a retreat location, possibly living outside, it will make a big difference to be clean and not smell horrible. If anyone else in the area notices how clean and odor-free you are, they will want to trade something with you to get their own soap and shampoo.

Fireplace Ash

There is a great story about American prisoners of war, held by the Japanese in World War Two. Several of the prisoners were sick from diarrhea, and were given no medicine from their Japanese captors. An enterprising American officer mixed water and fireplace ash and fed it to the prisoners who were sick with diarrhea, and the men were healed! The diarrhea went away!

That makes sense, because today on Amazon, you can buy charcoal pills that will help settle your stomach.

Besides mixing with water for diarrhea, and settling your stomach, fireplace ash has many uses.

Fireplace ash can be used in wounds, to kill bacteria and aid in faster healing.

Fireplace ash can be added to soil to help in farming. Adding it to soil injects nutrients, except nitrogen, back into the soil. It aids in increasing the pH level in soil, which helps plants grow. Plants that like calcium, like tomatoes, avocados, beans, peas, and spinach will be helped from ash added to the soil.

We add fireplace ash in our chicken coup, and the chickens promptly take a bath in it. The ash kills mites and bugs that feed on the chickens.

Bugs cannot stand fireplace ash. Pouring ash in the garden not only helps the soil, but also gets rid of parasites in the garden, like snails and slugs. You can throw some fireplace ash on an ant colony, and the ants will leave.

It is also good to spread fireplace ash in the corners of your house and cellar, as it repels mice, rats, and roaches. In the closet, fireplace ash repels moths.

Fireplace ash, mixed with vinegar, gets ticks, lice and fleas off of animals.

Anything Night Vision

This is probably the least-cheap item referred to in this book, hence its position towards the end of the book. But anything night vision is very valuable. In military language, a night vision device is a great "force-multiplier." Having something like this is analogous to being the only person with sight in an area full of blind people. It is extremely valuable, and gives you an almost unfair advantage of anything out there in the dark.

The cheapest one I could find was $400, but these things usually sell for up to $3,500. It is possible to get one on a rifle scope, but that is awkward to walk around at night with. The most useful ones I have found are monoculars.

PVS 14 seems to be the latest model out there, and at $2900 apiece, it is such a large expenditure that there is no way a short description here could do it justice. You need to study up on this, and get to know the advantages and qualities of this night vision equipment. The PVS 14 runs on a single AA battery, is waterproof, and can be attached to a helmet or rifle, or just held as a monocular.

But night vision is extremely valuable. It has occurred to me that nighttime always seems to be the time that predator animals go out to hunt for food. They find and kill something at night, then alternatively sleep and snack on the carcass all day long. So you can protect yourself and your livestock with some night vision technology.

And while hunting with night vision is illegal nowadays, in a situation where the law no longer exists, hunting with night vision technology would help keep you and your family fed.

I have also heard from people in the military that night vision is a huge advantage in movement. If you are trying to go from one point to another at nighttime, you can use night vision equipment to locate campfires and flashlights in the distance, where with your naked eyes you would only see darkness. Soldiers in Iraq have even driven their Humvees at night with all the lights turned off, relying only upon their night vision equipment to see the road ahead.

So while night vision is not a "dirt cheap" prepper item that should be repeatedly bought and stockpiled, I wanted to briefly mention it in this book, as the extreme advantage it will mean to anyone in an SHTF situation.

Things That Regenerate

Until now, we have mostly been discussing one-time used things. You keep a stockpile of something, use them once or trade them, and then they are gone. I want to spend a little time on some things that will help in a true SHTF-situation, and they will not run out. You use them, then you can use them again. Theoretically, the supply never ends. I call these things "regenerating things."

Off-Grid Power

Electricity can do a lot of things, like heat and cool your surroundings, give light during the dark, cook your meals, freeze food so that it stays good, and so on. Well, obviously. If at all possible, you should harness the energy that comes free from the sun, streams, or the wind, or a combination of all three.

Off-grid systems are modular, meaning that you can add or subtract sources of in-coming energy. And off-grid energy will require some equipment, besides the solar panels, wind turbines or water wheels that you will use to collect the energy. You will need to keep a bank of batteries hooked up, and a charge controller between the source of the energy and the batteries. The charge controller keeps the batteries from being over-charged.

Such a system will also need an inverter, which is a piece of equipment that changes the DC electricity that is stored in your battery bank to the AC electricity that will be used in your house. Just about all the items in an average household run on AC electricity.

It is also a good idea to have a generator that will turn on and charge your batteries when they are low in power. Back-up generators are powered by gasoline, natural gas, propane or diesel. Keeping the batteries at the same or similar charge will also make them last longer.

But here is a very important consideration with generators: the location of your generator needs to be safe. If it is inside a garage or structure where you might go, you could die from carbon monoxide poisoning. Carbon monoxide does not smell, and if it creeps into your house or dwelling, you won't know it until it is too late. For this reason, most smart off-grid homeowners and businesses keep their generators outdoors, and far away from any structures.

For all the equipment needed to generate your household's power off the grid, you can put the system together yourself, piecemeal, or you can get a company to do it for you. There are many companies out there that will help you take your house off the grid, or will help you in building your new house without a hook-up to the electrical grid. The quotes I have gotten for a small house, with everything included, start at about $30,000. While this is a huge amount, keep in mind that you will be free from the brownouts that happen to the grid, and the price increase that inevitably happen to everyone on the grid. And your electricity bill will be zero.

How long will all this stuff last before it needs repairing or replacing? In my own shopping around for this equipment, I believe it is safe to say that ten years is the longest a system can go before it needs repairs or parts replaced.

Seeds And Gardening

Of course, instead of living off of food that you have bought for storing, or bartering for other food, you can always grow your own new food. This requires a lot of land, good soil, seeds, and constant watering. Ideally, you will have a hilly piece of property where you can collect and store water at a higher elevation, then irrigate your gardens down below using gravity. And any garden runs the risk of being seen by people outside your property, or animals that would rather eat your crops than let you eat them. So you will need to protect your garden.

That also applies to animals that would like to dig tunnels underground and get to your plants. It is for that reason that every raised bed I build, after digging below grade, I first place hardware cloth, which is a strong screen down there, before I build the sides of the raised bed and fill it with soil.

Every time a vegetable is grown to be eaten, it is a good idea to collect and dry the seeds from that plant, so that the seeds can be used the following year to plant new vegetables. In time, packages of seeds may become a new thing to barter. Almost a new currency.

Rabbits

Rabbits are a great source of protein, very filling and, as with almost any other meat, taste like chicken. They are hearty, and they, well, breed like rabbits. It is possible to start with a small group of rabbits and keep them fed, only to have them multiply to become a big group before long. It would be a great idea for any serious prepper to begin keeping rabbits. Any meat that you don't need yourself could be used for barter.

Chickens

Chickens are great for eggs and meat, and require little care besides watering and feeding. The females, called hens, have a few years when they produce eggs, which are an excellent source of protein. After which, they are not useful for anything besides meat. The males, called roosters, make a lot of noise and are sometimes mean to the hens. But they are necessary to keep the flock regenerating, and they will protect the flock if any predator gets inside the chicken coup.

Another benefit of having chickens is the extremely-high nitrogen poop they drop. Chicken poop is sold at fancy gardening stores, but with your own chickens you will be able to collect your own. It is extremely smelly, and new chicken poop can burn plants. So it is best to age the chicken poop in vegetable compost for at least six months before you spread it around in a garden. And while the poop is composting, you should turn it over at least once a week. But once the chicken poop is aged and safe for plants, it is great fertilizer that plants love.

Aquaponics Systems

These systems look interesting. Basically, the idea is to have a group of fish, Tilapia, in a contained aquarium. Their poop is filtered out of the water by a solar-powered water filter, and then their poop is used to fertilize plants. One of the pants is Duckweed, which is good for humans to eat but is also fed back to the fish. A totally self-contained, regenerating system!

The type of fish used for these systems is Tilapia, because it is a pretty durable fish that will stay healthy and not die from the diseases that fish tend to dry from. Also, they breed pretty reliably, and they taste pretty good too!

Epilogue

So where does this all leave us? I hope that this book has established in you some mental priorities of buying your preparation supplies. There is a finite amount of money all of us have to devote to our prepper supplies, and we have a limited amount of time in which we need to prepare. Ideally, we could stock our own Walmart Superstore on our own raw land and ride out any disaster, no matter how long. But short of that, it is important to prioritize what we are able to stock up on, and what to spend on those preparation items. Also, we know some items to stock up on -- items that will be extremely important in a societal collapse.

Some good prepper habits are also important. Water, being the single most important item to have taken care of, should be stocked up on, and filters should be stored and over-stockpiled. Beyond that, keep up the opportunistic prepping. Whenever you are in a hardware store, keep a look out for sales on shovels, hatchets, axes, hand tools and 5-gallon buckets. Whenever you are in a Walmart store, make sure to always buy some salt, soap, athlete's foot cream and jock itch cream. Whenever you are in a grocery store, make sure to pick up a 2-liter size plastic bottle of soda pop for the family, and a few bags of dried pinto beans. That way, when the family finishes the soda, you can clean and dry out the bottle, then fill it with the pinto beans for storage. And while you are at it, pick up an extra case of bottled water, even if your garage is already half-full of cases of bottled water.

And on your way home from work, make an extra stop in the local Goodwill or Salvation Army store. Or garage sale. As I wrote earlier in this book, the clothing in those places, especially coats, may save your or someone else's life someday. And used board games and paperback novels will help keep morale up for your prepper group.

And keep an eye out for important prepper items sold on Ebay. Remember to watch for used sleeping bags, blankets and coats up for auction. Also, watch for auctions of knives and multi-tools that stupid people tried bringing onto airplanes and got confiscated. You can buy these items for very little money, by doing a search for "TSA" on Ebay.

And keep repeating all of these purchases. The items listed in this book are for collecting and over-stockpiling, so that if and when needed, you can use the excess to barter for other things you need but don't have.

And make sure to keep up the prepper education. Of course, buying and reading this book is a great start, but make sure to buy other books, listen to some great prepper podcasts out there, and watch some movies, TV shows and YouTube videos that have some great prepper information. Below are some notes that I have made on prepper education:

In my opinion, prepper education has to begin with one author. The mention of his name among preppers reminds me of that scene in the movie *Blazing Saddles*, in which a conflict is resolved by the phrase "You would do it for Randolph Scott!" Immediately everyone within earshot stops what they are doing and pays impromptu respects to the cowboy actor Randolph Scott. Hats come off. People almost look as if they are in prayer. The reverence is hip deep.

That is what it is like among preppers when the name James Rawles is mentioned. He is truly the Randolph Scott of this genre. He started it all, and made it acceptable to the mainstream.

I must confess that I feel the need to stand in respect while I even type the name James Rawles here. ALL of his books, both fiction and non-fiction, starting with *Patriots*, and lately with *Liberators* and *Tools For Survival* are helpful to people who see a societal collapse coming and want to be prepared. He even has a great website that started it all online: *Survival Blog*.

For those who are new to prepping, or even for those who are experienced preppers, Rawles' blog *Survival Blog* or any of his books would be a great place to start.

There are other authors in this genre, whether it is prepper fiction or prepper instructional books. Heck, I even have a prepper fiction book out there. But below is a very incomplete list of other authors whose blogs I read, podcasts I listen to, YouTube channels, TV shows and movies I watch, and I would recommend you do too:

In The Rabbit Hole. Are preppers hip? "Of course not," you might say, "we are all supposed to be like the Michael Douglas character at the end of the movie *Falling Down*." Well, let's face it, most of the time that criticism is spot-on. By and large, we preppers are a strange lot. But Aaron Frankel, Jason McConniel, and Jonathan Kanarek promote a different view of preppers with their *In The Rabbit Hole Urban Survival* podcasts. Based in Texas, the hipness and optimism of their podcasts are infectious. And the information contained is very helpful.

James Price runs a great blog at the website *Death Valley Magazine*. An honest-to-goodness civilian contractor who has worked in many of the world's war zones. Price has really been shot at and has even returned fire! He writes with a healthy skepticism and great sense of humor. You would be surprised how readable and enjoyable his blog is. He even offers weapons training, gear and "adventure tours."

Mark Goodwin has a great podcast at the *Prepper Recon* website. I have learned a lot of prepping skills and information from his podcast. He also has a great new book series out there, *The Days Of Noah*. I also like it that his blog has a Friday night movie featured, and a Sunday Bible sermon written by Mark himself. The *Prepper Recon* store also sells some cool prepper supplies, including first aid kits, back packs, and gun slings.

The *Prepper Recon* website also has a tab for "Coupon Corner" and I would highly recommend that you check it out. It is a treasure-trove of information and links that will help you stockpile many preps necessary for survival, and spend next to nothing on them. Literally. This part of the *Prepper Recon* website might be the best-kept secret in the online prepper world.

Jack Spirko also has a great podcast, at *The Survivalist Podcast*. It is an excellent podcast with many interesting guests, and Spirko has been at it longer than most others. He also offers training.

Bob Mayne has a great forum and podcast at the *Today's Survival* website. Mayne has a very down-to-earth approach to prepping. He has mentioned that he makes his podcasts so that you can play them for non-prepper family members and you won't be treated like a freak. For people who want to interest their skeptical friends or spouse into prepping, the podcasts at *Today's Survival* are a good and safe place to start. Mayne also has a great fill-in from time to time, Mexican Joe.

I have also been impressed with the podcasts at *The Preparedness Podcast*, run by Rob Hanus. Hanus also has a couple of interesting-looking books out there, *The Preparedness Capability Checklist*, and *Surviving EMP*.

Kyle, at *Rational Survival Blog* has a very informative series of podcasts. Still new but very promising. Kyle has a great phrase that describes his podcasts: "Are you preparing to be poor, or preparing to prosper?" To which I would answer, "Of the proffered picks, I persist to be primarily prosperous with my preps."

Rick Austin at *The Preparedness Radio Network* has very good podcasts. He also has an interesting book, *The Secret Garden Of Survival*, which instructs on how to grow a garden that will not be noticed by people nearby.

Zion Prepper has written a few good books on prepping, and his YouTube channel is filled with helpful prepping advice.

I also want to mention a couple of guys who don't have their own blogs or podcasts, but they appear on other podcasts a lot and they speak at prepper conferences from time to time. Nurse Pete (Pete Peterson) is an excellent resource of home remedies and medications. Nurse Pete is filled with very valuable information, on subjects from healing with aloe vera plants and cayenne pepper, to using Preparation H in ways you would not expect, and some good advice on fish antibiotics. Reportedly, Nurse Pete's suturing class in prepper conferences is routinely sold out.

Also, Geoffrey Lawton makes the rounds at prepper shows and podcasts, where he discusses his specialty, "permaculture." Geoffrey Lawton is the giant in the field of permaculture, which is a method of making the best use of soil and livestock, in such a way as to awaken and preserve the soil and maximize its output. He also has some great ideas on irrigating areas that appear to others to be a lost cause. He recently set up his own website, GeoffLawton.com.

Whoever is behind the YouTube videos at *Analytical Survival* does a great job, but he keeps his identity a secret. Whoever he is, he is a real dichotomy. According to an introductory video, the guy behind *Analytical Survival* is a former Green Beret who has a PhD in literature from UC Berkeley. If he doesn't educate you on MRE's and electrolyte replacement drinks, he can then explain to you the significance of *Crime And Punishment* in western literature.

Souther Prepper 1 has a great YouTube channel, and he has co-written a good book with Mark Goodwin, named *Retreat Security and Small Unit Tactics*. Southern Prepper 1 is also a consultant on the TV show *Doomsday Preppers*.

Prepared Housewives is a great blog with some great advice on all kinds of prepper issues, not just geared towards housewives. I have been especially impressed with this website's advice on canning, food storage and preservation.

I also like Bexar Prepper's YouTube videos. Very informative, and she includes a lot of good canning advice.

Dr. Bones and Nurse Amy have a great website, packed with a lot of great "survival medicine" and prepping advice, and it can be found at doomandbloom.net. Occasionally they have a podcast as well.

Scott Hunt recently wrote a great book on prepping, *The Practical Preppers Complete Guide to Disaster Preparedness*, which may become the standard on all sorts of prepping subjects. That book has some pretty clear written explanations and photos to explain prepping projects. Hunt also has a great YouTube channel, which can be found by searching "Engineer 775". Anyone who can put together a truck that is powered off of wooden logs needs to be paid attention to. In the past he has also advised the producers of the TV show *Doomsday Preppers*.

Other YouTube channels to watch: Maine Prepper, Sensible Prepper, 7 Trumpets Prepper, The Patriot Nurse, The Lord Humungus, Prepper Nurse, Healthy Prepper, The Buckeye Prepper, Zion Prepper, and The Urban Prepper.

I should also mention the *Conflicted* card game: this looks like a very good thing for family discussions. But kind of pricey: $18 on Amazon.

And, speaking of games, check out the *Doom and Bloom Survival Board Game*, which is expensive at $40 on Amazon, and *The Worst Case Scenario Game*, which is no longer being produced but can be bought on Ebay.

Movies and TV shows: the *Twilight Zone* episode, "The Shelter," from the third season, *Doomsday Preppers*, *The Walking Dead*, and the movie *American Blackout*. Don't forget to also watch the movies *Panic In Year Zero*, *Book Of Eli*, *Goodbye World*, *The Postman*, *Red Dawn*, *Cast Away*, *The Road Warrior*, and *I Am Legend*.

Made in the USA
Lexington, KY
20 May 2015